"For years I heard Coach Fred tell his story to advisors and leaders at Ameriprise. Now in his book, Fred takes a series of tragic personal events and shares his most intimate emotions during his darkest days. He deftly uses his story to teach us how to face our own life challenges. In the future, when I face difficulty, I will draw on Fred's lessons. I will connect with my friends and family in a more meaningful way. I will schedule that heli-skiing trip I dreamed about. As a leader, I will use Fred's teachings to be more compassionate and help others manage difficulty in a more effective manner. I will forever be thankful to Fred for his courage to take the most personal medical and family issues and turn them into positive life lessons. If you want to live a more connected and meaningful life, then this book is a must read."

-Bill J. Williams, Executive Vice President, Ameriprise Franchise Group/The Personal Advisors Group, Minneapolis, MN

"I had an opportunity to first hear Coach Fred speak at the 2013 National Leadership Conference. Besides our connection in both being from New Jersey, Fred's story of perseverance and dedication touched me to my core. I knew immediately that I wanted my advisors in Florida to hear his story and the first opportunity I could get Fred to Florida was for my Women's Retreat in July 2013. The setting could not have been any better. In a brief forty-five minutes, Fred was able to take us into his world of tragedy, despair, hope, fight, and triumph. It was an amazing journey of reflection and inspiration. Fred posed a very important question to everyone in the audience: 'What are you waiting for?'

Not a month goes by that I don't have someone tell me that the 2013 Women's Retreat had a profound impact on their thinking, and one advisor told me that it changed her life. Coach Fred was the glue that held that retreat together and he turned it from being a *meeting* into an *experience. Keep Showing Up* is a blueprint for how to overcome adversity and live a more enriched life; both for yourself and the ones you love."

-Brian J. Mora, CFP®, CRPC®, AWMA,®
Senior Franchise Field Vice President, Ameriprise Financial Services, Inc. (and Coach Fred fan!), Miami, FL

"I heard Fred as a motivational speaker years ago. I was working as an event marketing manager for a large company and heard Fred's presentation at a corporate team meeting. It wasn't his specific trauma that resonated with me but his reaction to adversity that moved me. When I first heard Fred say the words 'What are you waiting for?' I believed he was talking directly to me and I felt that I was meant to be in that place at that time. I scheduled a lunch meeting with Fred that same afternoon and asked how I could help get his message to others. Over the next couple of years, I had the pleasure to hear Fred deliver his speech at events across the country. Each time I heard from guests in the audience about how they felt the message was meant just for them too—phenomenon! Fred has an incredible way of making his story feel like a conversation with a friend. After reading this book, *Keep Showing Up*, I feel the same way; it was meant just for me—and everyone else!"

-Cheri Sabol, Wellness Marketing Specialist, Pilates Instructor, Personal Trainer, Minneapolis, MN

"There are few individuals who dare to really know themselves and what they want in life; who are willing to face their fears and who are willing to get uncomfortable for something bigger than themselves. There are few individuals who know they want to live their life with passion and purpose and who will do what it takes to accomplish just that. As a coach, friend, and client of Fred, I know he is one of the few. I am confident that Fred's commitment to helping others by sharing the lessons he's learned through his personal journey, coupled with his gift for storytelling, will inspire you and have you knowing without a doubt that you are incredibly special. Enjoy this amazing book!"

-Jean Hanham, MBA, PCC, Life Coach, JMH Coaching, Entrepreneur, That Real Estate Couple, The Villages, FL

"When we least expect it, life has a funny way of putting us in front of people who, at the time, we cannot foresee walking alongside us on the long journey ahead. I first met Fred in a cheap Jersey Shore hotel room following senior prom. We immediately sensed the adventurous spirit in each other and began what would become a decades-long friendship. Over the years, we grew close over a love of the outdoors, family, friends, and laughter. And while I would never assume to fully comprehend the depths of the challenges Fred has faced, I was there for his multiple (and understandable) descents into despair and the ultimate rise above. Along the way, through his actions he has inspired me to be vulnerable, authentic, and compassionate, both in my dealings with others and myself. In this book, Fred shares poignantly what he has learned about himself, and more importantly, the path to self-actualization. Whether you are facing that which feels insurmountable or are just looking for some straight-forward and practical advice on how to not just exist, but to thrive, this book is sure to both inspire and educate."

-Scott Hamilton, President, Future Stars College Counseling, Sacramento, CA

Keep Showing Up

A Seeker's Guide to Thrive

In Memory Of

In memory of William Goebel, Father Peter Funesti, Malia Behr, Marlene Maguire, Peter Stewart, Chase Kowalski, James Hamilton, Michelle Hirsch, Joseph DeGange, Blake Barker, and all of the bright souls we've lost too soon.

Keep Showing Up

A SEEKER'S GUIDE TO THRIVE

Fred Schuldt

Splendor Publishing
College Station, TX

SPLENDOR PUBLISHING
Published by Splendor Publishing
College Station, TX.

First published printing, September, 2018

Library of Congress Control Number: 2018966597
Keep Showing Up: A Seeker's Guide to Thrive
Self Help
1. Motivational & Inspirational
2. Personal Growth: Happiness

ISBN: 978-1-940278-28-5

Printed in the United States of America.

For more information or to order bulk copies of this book for events, seminars, conferences, or training, please visit SplendorPublishing.com.

Dedication

This book is dedicated to my family: my beautiful wife Lisa
and my amazing children, Sydney and Andrew,
my son and moon and stars.

Contents

FOREWORD --XV

PREFACE-- XVII

ACKNOWLEDGEMENTS ------------------------------ XXI

Introduction: *We're Going On a Journey*------------1

1: *Ten Feet Tall and Bullet Proof* ---------------------5

2: *Going Through the Motions* ---------------------- 17

3: *There's Never a Good Day to Get Cancer*-----27

4: *The Victim Wants to Take Over* ----------------- 37

5: *What are You Waiting For?*---------------------- 45

6: *It's Okay to Ask for Directions*-------------------- 51

7: *Find Out What Makes You Come Alive*--------- 59

8: *Not Cursed . . . Carried!* -------------------------- 75

9: *The Power of Our Stories* ------------------------- 83

10: *One Hill at a Time* -------------------------------- 91

11: *Survive and Thrive* -------------------------------101

12: *Show Up with All of Who You Are*------------109

Epilogue --119

"If you're not where you want to be,
what are you waiting for?"

-Fred Schuldt

Foreword

"**K**eep showing up" is good advice. And it's even better advice when the one sharing it has continually showed up again and again for himself and others—no matter the difficulty and no matter how long the trial.

Anyone can give advice, yet few really live out the advice they give. Fred does.

I've had the privilege to learn Fred's story first hand, and then to walk with him over several years of cultivating that story into meaningful words that would encourage and benefit those who read them. I think we succeeded.

Fred is the real deal. He's kind, big-hearted, raw, and real, and he's determined. He also knows almost instinctively what's most important in life, and he knows how to keep showing up for it.

As you get to know Fred and learn his story, you might be tempted to think that for some reason he's a bit stronger than most of us—maybe it's just his personality or built into his DNA. But that's not so. You'll soon realize he shed many tears and felt weak, small, and quite insignificant at times, as we all do when trials hit hard. Or you might assume that showing up was easy for him—second nature—and that he did it every time without question. But that's not so either. He thought about quitting, too.

At times, the events in life may catch us off guard. One day things can go the way we hoped they would, only to be followed by a day or many days of unwanted challenges. But that is the nature of the gift of life, and through it we can grow, change, and even flourish . . . if we know how.

If you've faced adversity or are in the midst of it right now, if you've felt like giving up or giving in, if you've labored in your mind to understand how what you're going through could possibly be "fair," then this book is the tool for you.

We have today, and with that comes the opportunity to embrace the gifts that are right in front of us, no matter how disguised they come. Maybe all we need is a little help to focus on what matters most, so we can *Keep Showing Up* with all of who we are. I believe that is precisely why Fred showed up for us—with his big heart and his fresh perspective—within the words of this book. Knowing Fred as I do, I am certain he would love to sit down with you personally, one-on-one, and tell you it's going to be more than okay and that there's something for you to embrace *today* that is far greater than you ever thought.

So here's my invitation: I'm inviting you right now to *show up* right here with Fred, who is certainly showing up right now for you. It's highly likely to be a match made in heaven—a partnership that will inspire you to *Keep Showing Up* full throttle in your own life, every day!

Margo DeGange, M. Ed.
Author, Speaker, Lifestyle Design Consultant

College Station, Texas

Preface

Having come through the dark tunnel of chronic illness, I now live each day in the pursuit of real connections that lead to living of a fuller, more meaningful life. I strive to view my wife and children with wonder at how incredible they are and how precious our time together is, rather than taking even a single second for granted. I work hard each day to be in the moment so that I can help my clients achieve peace of mind in the knowledge that they have a trusted advisor who cares for them on a personal level and can help them realize their dreams through planning and preparation. Because there's never a good day to get cancer, I share my story to raise awareness and motivate others to move forward after adversity hits: to understand the power of our words and deeds; to grasp the meaning of true connection; to recognize the power of an effective plan; to be able to tap into the simple wisdom that is all around us; and to find the endurance to transform our lives.

From my twenty plus years of experience in the financial services industry, helping people try to go from where they are to where they want to be, I've found that too many of us are waiting. We're waiting to live where we want or do what we want or even to be happy. We're waiting for when the kids are grown, when we retire, when our health is better, when we make more money, or when we hit the lottery. I've also seen that for way too many of us, that day never comes. We wait for retirement only to lose our spouse. The money we saved so that someday we could be happy doesn't mean so much anymore. We work so much that we're not with our kids. Then we achieve success, have more time and resources, and guess what? We missed it! They're grown; they're gone. What are we waiting for?

As a two-time cancer survivor, I've come to learn just how fragile our lives are and how we don't always recognize how razor thin the difference can be between health and sickness, between success and struggle, between happiness and crushing woes. And I've seen the power of connection in our lives and what it takes to dig down deep and get up again.

For years I've been asked about writing a book. At first it was the people I knew or those I met and shared some of my story with. They would say, "You've been through all that? You should write a book." Then, when I started to do motivational speaking, it was almost expected. A speaker needs a book, right? Several years ago I was toying with the idea and spoke to some people when I got some sage advice. I was told to wait a few years because the book I would write later on down the road—after speaking for a while—would be much better.

But that's not why I wrote this book. I wrote this book because after several years of speaking, other people's stories started to come back to me. Sometimes, several years after seeing me, my message was having an impact on people who were hitting hard times. People also reached out to me looking for guidance when they were facing adversity or cancer. Each time, my very simple advice and way of looking at things seemed to help. There is a power to just being a survivor. In some way, I give people hope. Somehow, my story helps people connect the dots in their own lives. And as more and more people reached out with the struggles in their lives or the impact my message had on them or their families, there came a day when I just could not wait any more.

What I hope you take away from this book is the skill to tap into the simple wisdom that is all around us. I consider it a guide to help us thrive as we survive the ups and downs of life.

I hope to inspire you to create meaningful connections as well as a process to allow you to go from where you are today to where you really want to be.

Acknowledgements

Thank you to all of the many people who have had an impact on me and made my journey possible. It's *our* story, not my story: to all of our family, friends, and neighbors, for keeping the mailbox always full and the phone always ringing; to my mother, who taught me to never quit; to my dad, for changing all of our lives through his hard work and dedication; to my grandmother Anne, for setting the tone for my life, that you work hard, play hard, love, and give back to others what you can; to my Aunt Carol, for teaching me how to be generous; to my big brother, Bill, for inspiring me to be better; to my in-laws, Ron, Jane, and Stephanie, for all of your love and support; to all of the doctors, nurses, aids, and assistants, especially Arelis, Liz, Dr. John Scheuck, and Dr. Christine Aquino—your care is the reason I'm still here; to my best friend, Scott Hamilton, who doubled his cell phone minutes the day I found out I had cancer because "Freddy is going to need to talk"; to all of the kids I coached, their parents, and all of my clients, for letting me in, especially Ashely, Rebecca, Lexi, Ryan, Sean, Tommy, Tomer, Matan, Shane, Joey, Jacob, Ethan, Ari, Alex, Adrian, Matt, Danny, Zach, and EJ—thank you for letting me love you like my own; to my coach, Jean Hanham, for helping me find Coach Fred; to Peter Funesti, for being our priest and our friend, and for anointing our lives; to my lifelong friend, Melissa, for loving me just as I am for all these years; to Jenn, Casey, and Kiera Hamilton, for giving me a home away from home in California, and sharing Scott every year so we can go skiing; to the advisors I shared space with for all those years, especially Joe Virgone; to Tom

North, Bill Williams, and all of the leaders at Ameriprise, who hired me, believed in my message, and allowed me to fly; to Marci Peyser, for all those times you listened when I rehearsed—my speeches would not be the same without you; to all my Jersey Boys, the memories of our antics are forever a source of pride and joy . . . I love *us*; to the many friends I've made along the way who always see the best in me and help me move forward, especially Todd and Adrianna Jeffrey, Brad and Cheri Sabol, Pat Consedine, Stu and Andrea Brietkopf, Jimmy Hamilton, Art Peyser, Charlie Clayton, Brian Mora, Michael Barker, Rebecca Kowalski, Scott Baker, Marcus Ranger, Roger McCoy, Eric Johnson, Seth Courtwright, and Charlie Part; to Doug Lennick and Bill Bacharack, for their expertise and sage advice; to my music teacher Michael Benard, for putting me on the stage all those years ago; to my soccer coach, Paul Martin, for inspiring me to coach; to my wonderful editor Margo, for helping find the best book I had inside; to my nieces Brooke, Amanda, Courtney, and Nikki, for bringing me lasting joy; to my children, Sydney and Andrew, who make me so proud and bring meaning and purpose to my life; and to my beautiful wife, Lisa, who stood in a church with me twenty years ago, having no idea what she was about to get into, and vowed to be there with me in sickness and in health, for richer or for poorer, and in good times and bad, and then she showed up every day and did just that.

We're Going On a Journey

I'm going to take you on a journey, one that was *my* journey, in the hopes that it will help you in some way and impact your life. What I've learned is how to keep showing up and how to show up every day with all of who I am for what matters most in my life. I am truly excited to share my story with you, but before we get started, I need you to know that I had no idea I was going to go through a process that would change how I think and feel and live my life today. I'm just a regular guy who likes people. I wasn't looking to create a whole new person or radically change the way I live. I just found myself trying to hold on and survive. I'm going to need you to hang in there with me for a little while because even though my story has a great ending, the story itself wasn't always so great.

Throughout these chapters I will share from the heart about how I got knocked down—spirit, mind, and body—and how I got back up again and again and again. I'll share with you all the mistakes I made and the lessons I learned . . . about trauma and adversity, about despair and hope, about getting help (relying on others), about taking control, about meaningful connection, about impacting others, about heartbreak, and about triumph and transformation.

My hope is that my story will help you connect the dots in your life, and that you'll be able to use my journey as a guide for transforming your own life, to live one that is fuller and more meaningful. The idea that just one person might get some small gift from these words, or that they might help *you* in some way to hang on and tap into the incredible well of the human spirit, and find the inspiration to keep showing up, leaves me in awe. I'm most excited because I know that from hearing my story you'll be reminded that where you are today is *not* where you'll always be, and *you* get to decide where you're going!

Notes of Reflection:

Chapter 1

Ten Feet Tall and Bullet Proof

I was thirty when it all started. I never thought anything would ever happen to me. I was ten feet tall and bullet proof. I think like most people, I believed bad things happen to others, not me, but there I was in the hospital bed fighting for my life. I thought, "How did I get here?" Everything was going so good. I was blessed to have a beautiful wife and a beautiful eighteen-month old baby girl. We were happy. We had just bought our first home. I finished my first year as a financial advisor and became an independent contractor. Wow, I had started my own business, one in which I could help people get to where they wanted to go. Yes, everything was going exactly as planned . . . and then it wasn't!

You see, I had diverticulitis and I wasn't taking care of myself. I was burning the candle at both ends, running my business, eating late at night, and not eating healthily. And I was stressed out. My wife and I had taken on three of the most stressful things you could do—and all at the same time—when we bought a home, had a baby, and started a business. Then to make matters worse, the late nineties tech bubble had burst, and business suddenly got a whole lot more difficult. And then somehow, the company from which I own a franchise realized they had over-paid me on some first year bonus; I went to work on a Friday, checked to see my compensation, and saw I had a negative $10,000 account. We would not get paid again for another three months—not until I could keep up with my expenses and get back ahead of the $10,000 deficit. Somehow though, we made it through. Somehow there was just enough each month to get by and stay afloat, but things were about to get worse—much worse!

The pain in my intestines was getting to be too much to handle, so I went to see the doctor. He suggested it might be time for me to have surgery on my intestines to take out the bad spot. I told him I didn't have time right now; I had too much going on. "Maybe in about five years," I said, "When my business is really grown." He wasn't convinced, so we scheduled a CT scan for the next week, and back to work I went.

Saturday morning came. My wife went to the gym while I stayed home with our daughter, Sydney, when suddenly the searing pain caused me to drop to my knees. I crawled to the phone. I was crying and Sydney was crying. I couldn't even think clearly enough to figure out where my wife Lisa had gone, so I called my parents. They hurried over. My mom looked after my daughter while my dad rushed me to the hospital. Every step was like a sharp knife in my stomach and every bump on the road caused more excruciating pain. I clenched my teeth and waited in the emergency room. I got in, saw the doctor, told him the pain was a ten out of ten, and he proceeded in making some big mistakes. He shot me up full of Demerol, saw that I was scheduled for a CT scan on Monday, and sent me home. Now I didn't want to be there anyway, so it was fine with me. Shot full of pain killers and feeling fine, my dad and I made jokes in the ER until they released me, and off to my home I went. On Sunday, we had a party for my Mom, and I was feeling worse by the minute. Monday came, and I put on my shirt and tie and went to work. The guys in my office were worried, in that I didn't look too good. Monday night, I drove myself over to hospital to have the CT scan. It turned out that I knew the technician—we went to the same high school. After the test was complete, he looked very nervous, and rushed off to get a doctor. The doctor told me I was quite sick and needed to be admitted. "When?" I asked. "Now," he confirmed. I said, "Yeah, but I'm in short term parking!" I went on, "But I need to see my baby tonight!" "No," he replied. "But I have appointments with clients tomorrow." "No," he said again. "Yeah, but I'm going skiing in Lake Tahoe this weekend!" He simply stated once more, "No."

Yes, bad things don't happen to us, until they do. I thought I was ten feet tall and bullet proof. I had a ruptured intestine. My body had been poisoning itself all weekend. I had peritonitis and was septic. I was worried about flying to California to ski, when I was about to be fighting for my life. I was so sick they kept me in the hospital for five days just to get me stable enough to do the surgery they should have done that Saturday morning when they sent me home. I was angry. Yeah, I didn't want to be there anyway and I gladly went home, but they're the doctors, how dare they send me home?

Friday morning came. It was time. After a fourteen-hour surgery and several hours in recovery, I was moved to a room late that night, and I woke up to the most incredible pain I'd ever been in. My whole abdomen was on fire. The pain was unbearable. Something wasn't working with the back shot they gave me and I begged the nurses to give me something else. There was a miscommunication with the anesthesiologist; the nurse gave me some pain killers she shouldn't have. There was yelling and fighting among the staff and suddenly it was all fading away. As I lay on the bed hooked up to all kinds of stuff I heard the long beep, and I somehow knew it was bad as the nurses rushed in saying, "Mr. Schuldt, you have to breathe!" Three more times that night I would stop breathing. It was so strange fighting to remember to breathe, then letting go and

7

hearing the long beep, and somewhere deep inside knowing I had stopped breathing as the nurses rushed back in to get me breathing again. I was scared. Not only did I have a wife and a baby, but my wife was four weeks pregnant. I was a financial advisor and I didn't have enough life insurance. All I could think was, "I don't want to be a famous financial advisor! If I die without enough life insurance for my kids, the advisors in my area will talk about me forever—the financial advisor who didn't have enough insurance. Great. That's not what I want my legacy to be."

The morning came. I had made it through the night. Looking back, it was one of the worst mornings of my life. I had been through hell. I had been opened up from my pelvis to my sternum. My internal organs and intestines had been pulled from the cavity inside of me and laid on a table next to me so they could be cleaned of the infection. The destroyed parts of my intestines had been removed. The surgery took fourteen hours yet they couldn't complete it. I woke up to find my worst fears were realized as I looked down at the wreck that was my body. Being too sick, with too much infection, they couldn't finish the surgery and I was given a colostomy. A piece of my intestine was sewn to a hole cut in my abdomen. Fifty-eight staples put me back together. There were tubes in my nose and down my throat, and three drainage sites with tubes hanging out. I was devastated and I was angry, and I had no idea how that anger would stay with me and impact me over the coming years. I had no idea how big the mistake I was making really was, because how you go into trauma has a huge impact on how you get out. I learned this lesson years later, but it is so important I had to mention it now.

How You Go In is How You Come Out

My uncle, Max MacPherson, spent thirty-five years working as a paramedic on the highways of New Mexico. Over those years he saved and lost countless lives in his hands. He knows more about trauma than anyone I have ever met. He explains it this way: "How you go into trauma dictates how you will get out, so it is very important to not go into trauma with any pre-existing baggage or expectations." So, as a paramedic and the first one showing up for a person in extreme trauma, he felt it was paramount for the paramedics to not carry any pre-existing baggage and expectations with them. That way they could best help ease the fear at the start of the trauma for the victim, and help get them on an easier path to healing and recovery. If a paramedic took baggage and expectations from one event to the next, they just could not last more than a few years in the job.

For the person suffering from the trauma, I envision it as an orbit. If we go into it angry, afraid, and frustrated, then the opportunities to get angry—the emotional hand grenades—will build up one on top of the other. Put yourself in my scenario for example: first you get diagnosed, then you go to the doctor for tests, your tests get delayed, you encounter problems with insurance, and you have to cancel plans and change routines to do treatments. Each obstacle presents an opportunity for you to get angrier and more frustrated, and the emotional orbit around the trauma will get tighter and tighter, and it will be extremely difficult to get away from it and move on to your healing. If we carry anger or baggage from one physical or emotional trauma to the next—as I did—then the weight of it will multiply and it will get harder and harder to get away from it. The weight will one day become unbearable.

Spiraling Into Trauma

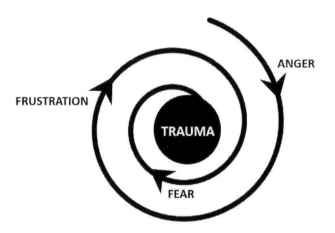

The great news is that if we go into trauma with patience and acceptance, knowing that many things will be out of our control, then we can avoid most of the emotional hand grenades. The anger and frustration won't build up and the orbit around the trauma will be looser, allowing us to circle away from the situation more quickly. Then we can heal. The best part is that we will carry less baggage forward. So, if and when we face trauma again, it will be easier to stay in a loose orbit and move on once again. Oh how I wish I'd known this all those years ago. I didn't, and therefore I carried anger and baggage for years.

Orbiting Around Trauma

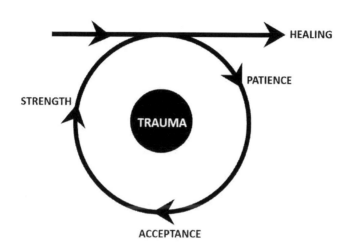

Trauma Model

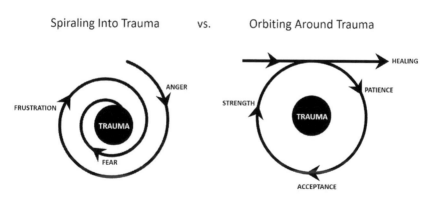

A Clear Difference

Attitude is Everything and the Only Thing!

I'll never forget waking up the second day after the surgery, when all that had happened and what I was going to have to contend with going forward really started to sink in. "Oh my God, what happened to me? How am I going to deal with this? I can't handle cleaning a colostomy bag!" I had fifty-eight staples holding me together. I had tubes coming in and out of every part of my body. Looking down at the monstrosity that was *me*, all I could think was, "I can't take care of this. I can't even see my own blood; I'm a fainter! I can't, I just can't." An open hole at the end of what was left of my intestines was coming out of me, sewn to a hole in my side and attached to a bag that would fill up with waste. I thought, "I won't be able to control it." What can you control if you can't control *that*? I was in pain, terrible pain, and I was angry at the doctors, angry at the hospital, and angry at the nurses. I was a *horrible* patient. I wanted to be left alone and so they left me alone. I hadn't been bathed or shaven. They had not even changed the bedding. I told my wife to have everyone stay away, and I lay there as miserable as I'd ever been in my life. And then an angel walked into my room, in the form of a nurse who emigrated from the Caribbean.

She took one look at me, her eyes welled up with tears, and she moaned, "Oh my Lord. What happened to you? Why have they left you here like this? Oh no, this won't do." She laid her hands on my head and my face and said, "I have three sons. No mother should see her son like this. Today you are my son." And I cried. She stopped her rounds and told the other nurses she would be with me for a while. She took my healing into her hands and ministered to me. She anointed me with her compassion and talked with me about how horrible the things were that had happened to me. She washed my hair and shaved my face. She cleaned my body with a sponge and carefully changed my sheets. She took lotion and massaged my back and legs, and I started to feel human again. As she was leaving I thanked her. She was having none of it and told me it's what any mother would do for her son. Then before she left she said, "It won't be easy, but you'll be fine my son. You're just gonna have to dig down deep and have a good attitude. Attitude is everything!"

I'm not sure why, but I never saw her again. Maybe her rounds never brought her back to my room. Maybe she took a few days off. Maybe there was something else, something unseen. I don't remember her name, but I'll never forget her face.

Yes! Attitude *is* everything. It's the most important weapon we have when we have to go to battle. It's also the only thing we get to control. When real adversity hits and you can't control anything, you get to control the most important thing—your attitude. How great is that? But it isn't always easy. It's a day-to-day, often moment-to-moment fight. And sometimes, until we can get it right, we just have to show up and try to find a way forward.

Find a Way to Move Forward

The next day I started to fuel the inner fire. I was never one to sit back and take it. I never backed down from a challenge. Raised in the seventies, I was taught that you face your problems head on. Life's gonna knock *me* down? Not without a fight! I had a lot to fight for: my wife, my daughter, my business, and my unborn child. I knew I needed to start really dealing with this. I asked my wife to bring my daughter in. I had not wanted her to see me the way I was. She walked in the room, carefully climbed on the bed, and held me.

I knew I needed to get home as quickly as possible. When the head nurse came, I informed her I was ready to learn how to take care of this thing that was coming out of my side. I couldn't put that on my wife. The nurse showed me how to clean it. I got up out of bed and walked. I ate for the first time. I sat up in a chair and shaved to feel clean. A couple of days later I went home. Almost thirty-five pounds lighter, and after thirteen horrible days of pain and sickness, I went home.

Three days later, because I had no choice, Lisa drove me to the office. Colostomy bag hidden under my shirt and tie, I held a pillow across my stomach to aid the staples in keeping me together. I limped into my office and leaned on the filing cabinets so I could gain the strength to make it down the hallway. I was there for an hour that first day and I went through the mail. The next day I showed up again, telling myself the whole way in, "You've got this, Fred. If anyone can do this, you can!" I listened to my music and looked for inspiration wherever I could find it, day after day, week after week.

After six months and several attempts to convince my doctor it was time to try the colostomy-reversal surgery, he agreed. I went back in—a little scared but mostly excited, and resigned to what I was going to have to deal with. The second time is harder in some ways. The first time I had no Idea how hard it would be. The second time I knew. I knew *too* much, really, and to have to give up control of your body knowing what is to come is not easy. And I started to get angry again. If they had done the surgery when they *should* have I wouldn't even being doing this again. I was still taking no responsibility for the decisions *I* had made that put me there in the first place! It turned out to be another fourteen-hour surgery. I woke up the next day with another fifty-eight staples holding me together once again. But the colostomy was gone. I was going to need to start over and heal again. But it was over. Or so I thought.

A week later I was out of the hospital, holding the pillow across my stomach on the way to work. I'll never forget that first day back. It was a Monday in September. I set a couple of appointments and got a referral from a happy client. I said to my friend Joe at the end of the day, "I can't wait for tomorrow! It's gonna be another great day and I'm going to get this thing really moving again." Well, tomorrow was not the day I thought it was going to be. Tomorrow was Tuesday, September 11th. It wasn't the day any of us thought it would be. When the news sunk in, I met my wife, we picked up our daughter, and we went home. I put up the flag and we prayed for our best friend, Susan, who was in the towers. We finally heard from her late that night. Unlike way too many others, she made it out. We were lucky. We live in New Jersey and can see New York City from our town. The next morning, even though we weren't ready for it, the sun came up, and we could see the giant hole in the sky where the twin towers used to be. I had to do what we all had to do and somehow, some way, find a way to move forward, and we did. As a nation, we did. Because no matter what happens in our lives, the sun comes up every day and we get a chance to show up. Sometimes we show up with all of who we are and sometimes we just show up.

Notes of Reflection: ....

Chapter 2

Going Through the Motions

Six weeks later my wife gave birth to a healthy baby boy. I had a son. It had been such a hard year and then . . . this! For me, it was a miracle. He almost never happened. We weren't planning to get pregnant when we did. If we had waited, he would not have happened. Somehow, the timing was perfect.

I don't think I realized at the time just how lucky we all were; it would take years for that to happen. If you had asked me at the time, I'd have told you that 2001 was the worst year of my life. Today, I'd tell you it was the best.

I had no time for anger and no time for deep thoughts. I decided not to sue. I did not want to live in the past, fighting some drawn out lawsuit. And the hospital was a Catholic hospital where my aunt had been a nurse and where my mom gave birth to both me and my brother. I'd gone there for burns and stitches and concussions. My Father had his successful cancer surgery there. No, I wasn't going to sue. I was too busy just trying to make it through each day.

I was already having problems. The surgery was not a complete success. Some days I could digest food and some days I couldn't. I was in and out of the hospital, and on and off a liquid diet. Looking back, this time was a blur. One long day led to another long night of pain. I would literally have to massage my intestines, pushing down on just the right spot so I could move food through the system and digest a small amount of it each day. I stopped wearing short-sleeved shirts.

At just over five feet, ten inches tall, I was down to 145 pounds. I was really starting to loathe my body and hate my being.I suffered through the night and talked myself through each day.

I don't know how, but we all have it inside of us to get up again. Being an American, I personally came from a long line of people who refused to give in. It's amazing what we can do when we have no other choice. What was I going do, give up? So we plugged along and made it through. The kids were growing up. My practice was growing little by little, but still, I was missing it.

I Was Missing It

Yes, I was missing it because I was never really present. I was always thinking about what I had to do next: the next phone call, the next meeting, the size of my next check. At home, I was thinking about the next day and the next set of bills. I was never in the moment. Thankfully, at the time, I wasn't stuck in the past but it was never about *now*. It was all about what was *next*. What's next . . . what's next . . . what's next, and several years just slipped by.

It was 2002, and soon 2002 turned to 2003. I skied that winter. It was good to be back. The country went to war and 2003 turned to 2004. My daughter started kindergarten. I started coaching, and 2004 turned to 2005. My best friend Scott and I went to Whistler, BC, one of the premiere ski destinations in North America. It was two giant mountains, one awesome village, and views like I could not have imagined. We were glacier skiing—incredible! I had earned it. Then my intestines knotted up and blocked. If I had been at home I would have gone to the hospital, but I decided I was not letting these damn intestines ruin this trip. I skied all day, and all night long I threw up whatever I ate. I even had a fight with

Scott—the only one we ever had. I flew home dejected, knowing I couldn't live like this any longer. It was time to see the doctor.

How Lucky am I?

When I got home I was admitted to the hospital. I met with my surgeon. He didn't want to do more surgery. The problems I was having were from all the scar tissue. I was so young when all the trauma happened that my body created a lot of scar tissue, much more than he was used to seeing with his older patients. "Thirty-year-olds just don't have their intestines rupture very often," he told me. He went on to inform me that I was going to have pain for the rest of my life. He added that if he did surgery on every patient who had pain after this type of surgery, he'd be in surgery all day long and never keep up, because each surgery causes more scar tissue, and round and round we'd go. But I was young, and he could see this was really holding me back, affecting my quality of life. "And you don't look good, Fred. You're too skinny." Not you *too*, Doc?

Since they couldn't just rush in and do surgery, that summer and fall I went for every test you could possibly imagine. If there was a way to look inside me, they did. It was months of waiting rooms and waiting for results. And I knew too much by then—way too much—so it was getting harder and harder to give up control of my body. I thought, "How many times do I have to go through this crap, and how much can one person take, and *why is this happening to me?*"

That fall, we went on a family vacation to Disney World with my parents and my brother's family, and my intestines blocked again! I couldn't let it ruin the trip. I didn't tell anyone, but I knew then that I was going to need more surgery. I couldn't take it anymore. I rushed through the park trying to get back to my family after getting separated for a while. I guess I cut

19

some guy off, and he said something to me; the next thing I knew I was in Disney World cursing some guy out!

Baggage and anger from the past was rearing its ugly head. A week or two later, Lisa and I were in the doctor's office when I found out it was going to happen. We picked a date: December 27, 2005. I wanted to get it over with as soon as possible so I could get healthy quickly and start my year off at work right. The doctor stepped out of the room to give us a moment. For the first time, I began to cry. Lisa looked at me and asked, "What's wrong?" "I can't believe I won't be able to ski again this winter!" I said. "What?" she replied, "That's what you're going to cry about?" "Yes!" I cried, "Because on the mountain I come alive, and I just can't believe I won't be able to do it again."

The morning of the surgery came, and I was not a happy patient. I was on time but the surgery was delayed. Angry, I went into my room to wait. I sat down and turned on the TV. It was the day of the big tsunami in Southeast Asia. Thousands of people were dying in the Philippians. For me, it was a wake-up call. "Oh yeah, you think you've got it bad, Fred? You're still here. You get to show up." And for the very first time in a long time, I said to myself, "How lucky am I?" My wife came in. I gave her a hug. In a daze, they took me off for surgery. I quietly thanked my doctor. "Don't thank me yet," he said. "We don't know what I'll find." I grabbed his hand and showed him the spot. I told him, "Whatever it is, it's right here. Look right here."

I usually wake up from surgery about an hour after it's done. The first thing I do is check the clock and try to figure out if the surgery went as planned. It never had before. But this time, could it be? Did it go more quickly than we thought? *Yes!* The knots were right where I showed him and they removed a foot of my intestines and took out some scar tissue, all without having to open me up. I had two small incisions and I was able to quickly go back to work right away. And over the next few weeks, I got better and better. It was a success!

I began to be able to digest food, and I put on a few pounds. I started wearing short sleeved shirts again. I was coaching the kids and growing the practice. It was over. Three major surgeries in four years and I had made it through. I wasn't going to miss any more. I wouldn't take it for granted. And little by little I became more present. I tried to be a better husband and father. I could finally breathe and I really started to heal. It was a good time in my life and for my practice. I wish it could have lasted.

Disney Picture-Perfect Family Comes Crashing Down

My friends would always joke with me, asking if I had another "Schuldt Family Barbeque" this weekend, or if there was a Hallmark card for the occasion of which my family was getting together! In our family gatherings, multiple generations got together—aunts, cousins, etc. We went on big Disney vacations, took family pictures everywhere we went, and were always there for each other. We were taught to stick together through tough times, and we did. We believed that family is everything.

Our family members were survivors. Our relatives came from Ireland and Germany and had fought for what they had. I was always one of the black sheep—one of the family rebels. In our family, crap rolled down hill. My grandmother sat at the top, my parents and aunts were next, then came the older cousins, after that my brother, and finally me. There was only one person younger than me; my cousin Lizzy. Her father died of ALS when she was just four years old (and I was six), and I wasn't going to mess with her. In fact, I was going to stick up for her. So the crap rolled down hill until it got to me, and then there was going to be a fight! I *never* backed down. To me that was a strength, but sometimes—as I was about to learn—our strengths can certainly become our weaknesses.

The whole story of what we went through is not mine to tell, but the Disney picture-perfect family was about to come crashing down and I was right in the middle of it.

On a family vacation in Vermont, I found myself in a huge argument with a family member who had lashed out at me over something really small; when I tried to find out what it was that was *really* going on, that person flat out lost it on me. With children in the room and my parents watching, two fists were put up next to my face in a rage and threats were hurled at me. In response, I got angry and said some things I shouldn't have. Between the two of us, awful words were exchanged—the type of things you just can't take back. False accusations and even physical threats were made against me. It was a real scene.

The next day, everyone tried to act like nothing had happened. When I said we needed to talk about it, that same family member who fought with me the day before flew off the handle again, and I was physically attacked with some of the children standing around to see it. It ended with that family member leaving with their family, and everyone else feeling heartbroken, confused, and upset. The rest of us tried our best to have a fun vacation, and not let my children or my young niece be affected, but we were all devastated. Our family had just been destroyed in a single day.

We returned from vacation but my parents and I were still quite upset. After work on Monday, while I was sitting in my office thinking about it all and trying to figure out why I was involved in the whole thing, I was struck with the idea that I must be right in the middle of it because I'm strong enough to handle anything, so I'm the one here to deal with putting us back together again. I left work and drove to my parent's home to tell them not to worry, that I was in the middle of it for a reason and that I was going to do whatever it took to face it head on and make it right. Just as I finished talking with them, my wife Lisa called and asked me to come home; she said she had something to tell me. When I stepped inside I immediately shared with my wife why I had been at my parent's house and how I was going to face the problem head on and make it right. That's when she revealed she had some information that was given to her first hand, and she proceeded to tell me what was *really* going on with the person who had attacked me. When I heard it, I dropped to me knees and cried. It was explosive and scary. It was not the kind of thing you would want to learn about a person in your family. It turned out that the family member who was so angry at me that night had been deceiving another member of my immediate family for the longest time in the worst way, and the one being deceived did not even know it. But now I did! If I did anything with this information it most certainly would tear our family apart. If I did nothing with it and it came out later in another way, and destroyed our family, I could never live with myself. It was a huge responsibility.

I went to see a crisis intervention counselor to get some advice, but no one could tell me what I should do. Yet I knew my relative was headed for more difficulty. I was raised to look out for my family, to protect them from harm. If I said something there would be trouble; if I didn't there could be even greater harm. I was burdened with so many thoughts. How could I live with myself? What would my grandmother say? What if something bad happens to my nieces and goddaughters? I had never backed down from a fight and I wasn't going to start then! I was taught to face problems head on, so I told the person what he really needed to know. At first he listened but could not hear. We met again several days later but denial took him over. I was accused of making it all up because of the fight in Vermont, and told I was trying to destroy his family, so therefore I was being kicked out of their life. What? Making it up? I said, "Do whatever you need to do but please, don't involve the rest of the family." It was too late—he'd already told my parents what I'd "done." I said to him, "Don't you understand? If I have to tell them what I know, they are going to believe *me*!"

That night my father called and wanted to talk. I explained that it wasn't going well and that it would take more time to fix things after the fight. He told me he knew what was going on and that he understood I would never do what I was being accused of. I drove over and told my parents the entire truth— what they did not need or want to hear. Well, now it was out and people believed me, but it was easier and much less painful for everyone to act like nothing had happened. Too much had transpired for things to ever be the same, but everyone wanted what we had in the past, and against the professional advice we received and against everything I'd ever been taught, a decision was made to sweep it all under the rug. I was obligated to attend a farce of a meeting where the real issue was not talked about and nothing was resolved. Fake apologies were forced out about the fight in Vermont, and we were all expected to keep getting together just like before, but the bond was gone. In my mind we were dooming ourselves to be a family that was no longer close and honest with each other—one that was fake, with underlying and unseen passive aggression. How was this healthy for my children? I was angry. I felt betrayed and left out to dry. What if I was attacked again? What if my kids were there next time? You want me to put them at risk and hope it doesn't happen again? I thought we face our problems head on! We don't sweep them under a rug. You lied!

Yes, I was angry. I was angry and that anger led me all the way to self righteousness: after what I did for them? How dare they? Looking back now it's easy to see that it really was no one person's fault. We all found ourselves in a very difficult situation. When there is pressure on a foundation, the cracks start to show. For about the next year and a half, we were forced into a pattern where we still got together but it was terribly awkward and unhealthy. It became a battle of wills. The person deceiving us all knew that I would never back down. I would never admit to the lie that I had "made it all up." I would never stop showing up for my family. I believe that is the real reason the information was given first hand to someone very close to me—my wife. Eventually, the entire truth came out and we were all free from the lies and deceit, but the family bond was truly broken. I had no idea what losing it would mean and how soon I would need it. I had no idea how emotionally stained and mentally exhausted I was. The physical battle I'd been waging for years had just added a new and extremely difficult layer as I was now fighting an emotional and mental battle as well—and just when I was going to need to be stronger than ever, before I was at my weakest.

Notes of Reflection:

Chapter 3

There's Never a Good Day
to Get Cancer

Fortunately for me, each year my beautiful wife Lisa sets an appointment for me to have a physical. She makes sure it's in my calendar, knowing that if it's my calendar I'll get it done. If it's not, then . . . .

It was now the winter of 2005. I was about to head back out west for my annual ski trip and just before I left, I went to see my doctor. She's a family doctor who had taken over her mom's practice. Her mother had been my grandmother's doctor, my parent's doctor, and was my doctor growing up. She knew our entire family medical history.

We went through a normal exam and she started to take blood. Suddenly—as if it just hit her—she said, "You know, with a family history of prostate cancer, you should have a PSA when you turn forty. I know you're only thirty-seven, but you're sitting here. Maybe we should do our first one." I said, "Same blood?" She said, "Yeah." "Well go nuts, doc," I exclaimed. And then off to my ski trip I went.

It was a great trip. It always is. The timing could not have been better. I had needed to get away from the ongoing family drama. My intestines were good, and I had a great time. I skied pretty well and came home with my battery recharged. I went to work on Monday, ready to grow the business again. When I got home Monday night, Lisa told me the doctor had called.

She wanted to talk to me about the results. Really? She never calls about my results. So I called her up. I asked, "Doc, the prostate?" "Yeah," she said.

So I went in and had a biopsy. It came back negative. "Don't worry, you'll be fine," she assured me. "Come back in six months." So I went back to my life and tried not to worry. By this time I knew it was all out of my control. And by this point I had already learned to focus on the opportunities I still have in life, not on the obstacles. So I went to my dad with an idea. Even *our* relationship was affected by the family stuff. We had always talked about getting a little boat when he retired. So I asked him, "What are we waiting for Dad?" He'd had cancer— still did in fact, and I maybe had cancer. At the time I thought, if we have twenty more years together, let's fish all twenty. Why wait ten? What if we only have ten? We'll miss it. What if we have less? So that winter we bought a little boat and got excited for the spring.

I had my second biopsy. It came back negative. "Don't worry, you'll be fine," came more reassurance from my doc. "Come back in six months." We spent a lot of time down on the Jersey shore that spring and summer on the boat. My son was four and my daughter was six. They loved it. We'd go for overnight stays. The kids would sleep in the boat. I'd stay up half the night tinkering around, trying not to worry. What if this is the only summer we get?

In September, I had the third biopsy. Everyone else said no, I couldn't possibly have cancer—not after everything I'd been through. I thought, "Yes, I can. What does one have to do with the other?" I knew deep in my heart, it was coming . . . I knew too much. The numbers don't play out well for prostate cancer if you're diagnosed when you're young. They don't leave you any choice; they take out the prostate. We get the news. My response: "So when are we doing the surgery, Doc?"

28

Lisa and I were walking down the hallway. She was crying. I hadn't heard her cry since her Grandmother died. Oh my God. I have cancer. Who's gonna walk Sydney down the isle? Who's gonna teach Andrew how to ski? Lisa's crying and I'm scared. I was already a fighter and I already knew what it took to survive. I knew that when real adversity hits and you feel like you can't control anything, you've got to control your attitude. You do that by focusing on the opportunities and not the obstacles. I also knew you can't do it alone. You've got to rely on other people. But I was scared because I knew how much energy and determination it takes to fight, and this time I knew I had nothing left in the tank. I called my best friend Scott and gave him the bad news. I told him I was scared. He told me I was just going to need to dig down deep. I said. "I won't be able to handle it this time. There's nowhere left to dig."

As the people in our life learned I had cancer, they would say things like, "What? With everything you've been through already? What a bad time to get cancer." And I would say "Yeah, yeah, bad time to get cancer." And in the back of my mind I was saying, "What? Bad time to get cancer? Are you kidding me? There is *never* a good day to get cancer" (or lose a loved one, or have someone get sick, or lose a job)! There's *never* a good day for adversity. That's what makes it adversity.

Well, you have to wait six weeks after a biopsy for your prostate to heal before surgery. So we took the kids to Disney World with my parents, because that's what you do, right? You try and make as many memories as you can. We had a good time—all things considered.

Three days later, in November of 2006, I went in for my fourth major surgery in six years. I was talking to the doctor before the surgery, telling him I was nervous. With the robot they use for precision cuts that will limit the side effects, they have to go through the abdomen to get to the prostate. I had all that scar tissue. There was a chance they would have to open me up if they couldn't get through. The doctor promised me he won't open me up—I've already been through too much. "Don't worry, Fred. I've done this surgery on a Vietnam vet who got shot in the abdomen and had a previous bowel resection." "Yeah doc," I said. "But I've had three."

I woke up after the surgery and looked at the clock. Something was wrong. I should have woken up five hours before. I was in terrible pain. The two-hour surgery had taken seven. Doctor Scheuck had kept his promise. He had to stop and start multiple times; they could not get through all the scar tissue. His team was ready to give up and they suggested he open me up. He said "*No*! I made a promise. This guy has been through too much." So they kept at it. But they had to do a lot of work in there—and there was a lot of bleeding, and my catheter got blocked. That was the pain I was feeling. But the doctor had gone off late to another surgery at another hospital and could not be reached. They could not do anything to me without his direction. The pain got worse and worse. Hour after hour I felt like my bladder was going to explode. Eventually I was crying, begging them to at least let my wife in to see me. They let her in for a moment. I was so angry. "I can't even get Cancer and have it go right!" Finally, the doctor came back, and *he* was angry—how could they leave me like this? He pushed down with his hands on my bladder to try and break the block, otherwise he'd have to get in me again. He pushed down hard, and I screamed in pain. The blockage came out. They sent me to a room. It was now two in the morning. I should have been back in the room comfortably resting at 2 *in the afternoon*! At eleven the next morning they sent me home. I was thirty-nine buy felt eighty-nine. I felt like I'd been hit by a bus.

On the Couch Again

There I was, on the couch again. This surgery, which was supposed to have been easy, was anything but. The seven-plus hours on the table with my head down by the floor and my feet up in the air caused all the anesthesia to pool into my shoulders and led to tremendous stiffness and pain. Knife-like pains shot into my abdomen from scar tissue that had been cut away and the swelling from the blockage in the catheter that was still there. To top it all off there was pain like I've rarely felt where my prostate used to be. For the first time ever, I took all of the prescribed pains meds and laid in a stupor on the couch, with our puppy, in the dark—watching old World War II movies I had watched with my dad growing up—just waiting for the next six hours to go by so I could take another Percocet and kill the pain. I didn't know if the cancer was gone. It would be six months until we knew that. I didn't know if I'd ever have sex with my wife again. It would be at least eighteen months until we would know that. It was a dark two weeks, but I had to get up. *Again*, I had to go back to work, and I did not want to miss another ski trip.

Yes, that's right. I was worried about my skiing again. On the mountain I come alive and, it's mine. I do it just for *me*. If I was going to ski that winter I would need to run. If I was going to run I'd need to walk. If I was going to walk I knew I'd better get off the couch. So the fighter in me got up, and wearing a diaper, took the dog for a walk. I tried to run a little. I wet my pants after two steps. I went home. *Ugh*. The next day I went for a walk, and took four steps before I wet myself. The next day it was eight, and the next, ten. Four weeks later I was running. Four months later I made a triumphant return to my happy place.

In the time leading up to the surgery, when I was stressed out from having some horrible and embarrassing test, or when I was waiting for results, I started visualizing a specific run that I'd skied and loved: the Stage Coach lift on the Nevada side of Heavenly Mountain. I would picture myself getting off the lift, dropping in to a little stand of trees, hopping back out, and blazing down the trail, jumping back off into some perfectly spaced out glory trees. I pictured deep snow, turn after turn after turn. It helped me get through some tough days. So when I was there again, not knowing if the cancer was gone but having a chance to ski it again, it was triumphant, but only for a moment in time. It did not last or lead to a major shift in my thinking or healing. It was just a little gift given to me that would help me get through and move a little further along.

But really, I was still stuck: stuck in the trauma, stuck in the past. I may have gotten up for a moment but it would not last. The surgery affected my sexual function, my mood, and my energy. For two months, I had to wear a diaper. I got home from my first run and told Lisa I was ready for the pad the doctor told me about—that I wanted to get out of this diaper. She bought them the next day. When I got home from work I was ready to try them out. She told me they were in the bathroom. I went in and saw a pink box ... hmmm, feminine pads. "Honey, are these *yours*?" I questioned. "No," she said, "They're *yours*." That's right. And there I was, all excited to get to wear *this*? I thought, are you kidding me? I mean seriously, this is just a slap in the face. I'll never be able to have another child. I may never have sex again. My prostate is gone. My seminal vesicle is gone. No fluids for the sperm, no more ejaculation. This sucks. I'm changed. I'll never be the same.

And I was struggling to do what I really needed to do. What, rely on the other people in my life? If I told people I was struggling, they were like, "What's wrong with you? You survived." And you know what? They were right. But surviving was not a lot of fun. I'd been surviving for eight years. Surviving sucks! Yes, it's better than a pine box. Believe me, I get that. But I did not want to just survive any longer. I wanted *more*. I was angry, and I felt guilty for not being more. Focus on the opportunities? I saw no more opportunities. All I saw were the many obstacles I'd hit and all the others lined up in front of me. The last straw was coming; I was going to finally hit rock bottom. I had done it to myself and I was doomed from the moment I said it.

I Was Doomed From the Moment I Said It

Attitude is everything and the only thing. I knew that but somehow I had forgotten it. And the day I told Scott that I couldn't handle it this time was the day I doomed myself to fall down. I said it out loud; I put it out there that, "There is nowhere left to dig." The words we use are so powerful. I had lost the fight and the fire inside that made me who I was. I knew it, but I had no idea what to do about it.

So I just went through one day at a time, never really happy—just sort of rolling along. I eventually had fair control of my bladder, but I had to wear those feminine pads for months and months. I had severe sexual dysfunction from the surgery and failed every time we tried. The pressure was building.

The surgery had taken out the cancer but it would take four years of heightened testing until I could be called *cancer free*. Cancer cells could have gotten out before it was removed. Only time would tell. The depression grew. I was going to work and coaching, and fishing with my dad and my children. I was here, but once again, not really present.

And then it happened. The global financial crises hit, and everything I had worked so hard for, and so many years to grow, was crashing down, because of greed and fear. My clients, who I care so much about, were watching their life savings come crashing down, month after month. They needed to hold on, for a better day to sell. I was the one they relied on. I was the one who was supposed to help them sleep at night. People were angry. I lost a few clients. And as the stock market continued to spiral down from 2008 into 2009—and hit rock bottom, so did I. Spirit, mind, and body... done! I was down and out. I couldn't breathe, couldn't eat, and couldn't sleep. I was falling apart. I lived every day in fear, just waiting for the bottom to drop out for me, my health, and my clients. When I should have been making phone calls to calm people's fears, I was stuck in my office and didn't even want to answer the phone. When I needed to be my strongest, I was at my weakest, and the victim inside of me wanted to take over.

Notes of Reflection:

Chapter 4

The Victim Wants to Take Over

When you find yourself asking "Why me?" just know that is the victim inside that wants to take over. When you start to doubt yourself and your self worth, that is the victim inside. When you start to loathe yourself for all your weaknesses, for being inadequate, for being damaged...victim! "What's wrong with you, Fred? What happened to the strong person you always were?" I had prided myself on being strong. The guys at my office would always compare me to the old blow up clown toy with the weighted bottom, when you knocked it over, it bounced right back up. They used to say that was me.

When I was eighteen months old, my parents bought their first home. I was a bit of a handful to say the least. On the first day after moving in, when my dad had gone to work, my mother put me in the play pen in the back yard she was so happy to finally have. It had a fence and a gate, and I was in the pen. It was a hot day and she went to the kitchen to get some iced tea, figuring she could leave me in the play pan for a minute. By the time she got to the front of the house and opened up the refrigerator, there I went, in my diaper, right down the street. I jumped out of the pen and unlocked the gate and went chasing after the other bigger kids in the neighborhood. After that, she says there was really no stopping me.

When I was twelve, I fell off my bike and had fourteen stitches in my shin. It was soccer season and I was going to

37

have to miss a game. I was not happy. My parents had a wedding to attend, and one of the other moms was picking me up for soccer. I put on my uniform, taped two shin guards to one leg, and told the mom and the coach that the doctor had said I could play. In the second half they had to stop the game. All of my stitches had ripped and I was bleeding all over the place. "I think maybe I'm going to get in trouble," I said.

That Freddy was gone: the Fred that had battled through all those surgeries and kept showing back up, the one who refused to give in and kept on skiing, the one who—even with cancer—wouldn't stop coaching kids . . . the happy, confident guy I was before all this started? Gone. I had lost hope.

Hope comes from being able to remember that where you are today in your life is *not* where you'll always be. That *this* is *not* it, and that in the end you get to decide how it will be. When you start to believe that *this* is it, that it's never going to be different, and that this is all life will ever be, you've lost hope. I had lost hope. I had lost *me*. I hated this new me. I knew I was never going to be the same, and I started to believe I was cursed.

What Have I Done to Deserve This?

A few years earlier a colleague of mine walked into my office just after one of my surgeries. I had come to the office in a sweat suit to go through the mail and my email inbox. She wanted to remind me of dress code we all agreed to. I told her I was just back from surgery and would only be in my office for a short time. I'd make sure none of her clients saw me. Then she told me that the reason I was going through all of this "stuff" was because I clearly wasn't living the life I was supposed to, so God was punishing me. Yes, she really did. A fellow Christian put those words on me. At first, I was angry, but slowly over time, they started to sink in. The words we use and the words we give to others have power, and I started to believe I was cursed and being punished. How lowly I must be for God to treat me like this. How could I love this me when clearly even God didn't? In church, my head was always bowed. I could not even look at the alter or sing the songs. Did God even want me here?

This was the final piece of the crash for me. My body was done. My mind was done, and now my spirit was wrecked and my faith was almost gone. What a kick in the pants. Springfield College was right?

I'm a graduate of Springfield College in Massachusetts. It was originally a YMCA teachers college. The symbol for the school is the YMCA affiliated triangle. It was on everything. It represented the school's Humanics philosophy of spirit, mind, and body. It teaches that all three are central to our health and happiness and that all three are connected. You build up all three together, and if one is down, all three will be down. My friends and I who lived off campus and partied used to joke about it; we called the kids who were really into the school, "Traingles." We'd joke about the spirit–mind–body connection it represented. It turns out, the joke was on me. What was once a joke was now becoming more powerful than I could have ever imagined. So *this* is why I'm not me? What was once a physical battle, turned into a mental battle, and then into the biggest battle of all, the spiritual one. Maybe they were right.

I Wanted to Be a Three. Why Not Me?

Sitting in my urologist's office waiting for the results of a six-month PSA check up, I glanced up and saw a Cancer Patient magazine. It was not something I normally picked up. Cancer was something I was trying to get away from, not something I was interested in reading about. But on the front cover there was a title of a feature that read, "Traumatic Transformation." I was intrigued and wanted to know what that was about.

There were some folks who had done interviews and put together a corresponding study from the findings about people who had survived major trauma in their lives. What the study showed was that people who had been through real trauma tended to fall into one of three groups. The first group made up a small percentage of the total. They were people who went through something horrible and were instantly changed for the better. You know the ones I'm talking about: they almost glow with life—those amazing people who allow the trauma to serve as an instant wake-up call, and they start living fully and are happy and actively engaged with others, always positive, strong, and grateful. They become unbreakable and go out to change the world. Well, that clearly was not me.

The second group—which was the largest—was made up of people who went through real trauma, glimpsed the changes they could make and how life could be different, but fell back into the old habits and their old ways. This group is likely to never feel the same level of joy and happiness again. They end up changed but not changed for the better.

The third group is also a small group. These people go through trauma, glimpse the changes they could make and how life could be, but fall back into their old ways and habits, lose their joy and happiness, and then fight for it again. They go on a journey to make the changes they glimpsed, start living a fully and more meaningful life, and become happy, strong, and confident. They tend to get fully engaged with others and start to make a difference in people's lives, and by force of will, they transform.

I sat there in the doctor's office stunned. I'm clearly not in group one, so I have a choice to make. Am I going to be forever damaged? Or am I going to change for the better and fight for it?

Reminded There is a Warrior Inside

So there it is. It's that simple. The way I see it is that it really all comes down to this: when life knocks us down we get to make a choice. We get to decide the outcome with our actions. What we decide to do after adversity kicks our butts will decide our fate. We can lie down and take it or get up and fight for it. We choose to be happy, or we choose to be miserable. We choose to be a fighter or we choose to lie down. We choose to live a full and meaningful life or we choose to just take what comes our way. We grab a chair right in the middle of the banquet of life and drink it all in, or we stand on the side waiting for someone to give us some scraps.

As I sat there waiting, I started thinking that I was just going to have to fight again, but the victim inside still wanted control. I had nothing left in the tank to fight with so what was I going to do? Where was I going to find the energy I knew it took to fight? Looking back, it's amazing how just when I needed it most, when I was at the end of my rope, some of the pieces would suddenly start to come together.

Still stunned from reading about the idea of traumatic transformation, the doctor called me in. We caught up and he told me the results were good. There was no sign of cancer yet. He asked about my sexual function and bladder control. I said they were okay at best. He told me to hang in there; he had to do so much inside me, and we did have those complications, so it was just going to take longer than normal. He asked how I was doing and fortunately I had the courage to tell him that I wasn't doing well. I really wasn't. And then he said something I'll never forget: "I know you've been through more than anyone should, but you're a bodhisattva and you can get through anything."

Bodhisattva? Well, I did not know what he was talking about, and he could tell. He told me that in eastern culture a bodhisattva is a warrior, but more of a spiritual one. It's someone who learns from the trials and battles of life and then works to help others live fuller lives. "That's you, Fred. You fight and learn how to survive and then you guide the rest of us through it."

My eyes filled with tears. I didn't feel like a warrior anymore. But somewhere deep inside his words rang true, and as I drove home I started to think, "You know what, he's right! I don't know about this idea of leading others, but *I am a warrior*. People are counting on me. It's time to put on the war paint. It's time to fight again."

I'd made a very important decision, one that would ultimately change my life. But deciding isn't enough. I was going to have to jump.

Notes of Reflection:

Chapter 5

What are You Waiting For?

There's a story I once heard. There was an old man riding his bike down the road near a small pond. He glanced over at the pond and noticed three frogs just sitting on a log. As he passed the pond, one of the frogs got in position as though he had decided to jump. The old man then looked back at the frogs, and guess how many of them were sitting on the log? All three, because there is a big difference between deciding to do something and actually doing it!

Yes, it was great that I had been reminded that I really was a warrior and it was awesome that I had decided to fight again. But that wasn't enough. I was going to actually have to *do* something and begin to fight. When you're at rock bottom, you can stay there or do something. It was time for me to get off the log and *jump*!

Fortunately for me, within a couple of days I was on the phone with my best friend Scott. I was telling him how I was still struggling, and he must have tired of hearing it and had the courage to say, "Freddy, I get it. You've been through so much that it's perverted. But I gotta ask you something. What are you waiting for? When are you going to do what you do? When are you gonna get up and fight? Do you think maybe it's time to get help?"

I didn't have a good answer for him. We hung up the phone. What are you waiting for? What a powerful question. I sat at my desk and then I started to dig down deep. Yeah, what *am* I waiting for? When *was* I going to do what I do and get up and fight? And I started to get a little mad. Not angry at the world but mad that I wasn't fighting for myself. I'd been fighting for my wife and my children and my family and my clients, and it still wasn't enough. I still hit rock bottom. And you know what? *I am* a fighter, *I am* a warrior. And I am good person. Don't I deserve happiness? Don't I deserve a great life? Don't we all? And if I really want to be a great husband and father then I need to love myself again; I need to be *whole* again. I thought about my grandmother and knew it was time to make a path.

Directing the Change You Can't Control

You see, years earlier I had gotten a call from my grandmother. She needed my help. When Grandma called, you went. She wanted me to take her to the outdoor store to buy some pavers. Now, Grandma lived in an apartment complex and I'm not sure why she needed pavers, but when Grandma says she wants something, you don't ask. When we got back to the apartment I was sent to the basement to get her gardening tools. "What's up, Grandma?" I asked.

As it turned out, there was a flower patch between the two buildings in the complex and there was a set of stairs that lead down to the parking lot. Over the years things had changed in the complex and younger, busier people had moved in and they had started cutting through the flower patch to get to their cars and were trampling on the flowers. My grandmother had put up a note in the common area, but they didn't stop. She talked to the super, but they didn't stop. She then put up a sign in the flower patch, and they didn't stop. And I'll never forget seeing this little old lady down on her knees—kneeling on a pad with her little flowered garden gloves—look up at me and say, "There comes a time when you have to stop resisting change.

46

Admit that it's here for good and then *direct the change.*" So she built a path through the flowers, and the busy people no longer trampled the flowers to cut through to their cars on the path. Yes, when change has come and won't be stopped, we have to direct the change onto a better course.

So I sat there that day saying, "Today is the day. When are you gonna do what you do?" I knew I had to get up and I had to direct the change I could not stop. I knew I had to get up for all the people in my life who were counting on me. I knew I had to be there for them, but *now* I found I was saying to myself, "Get up; you deserve a great life. You deserve it. Get up for *you*! Go and do what you do best." And I realized, no one was going to be able give me the answers. I was going to have to find them myself. And then it hit me: "Do what you do!"

Spirit, Mind, and Body Planning

"Do what you do." Yeah, that's right. I just need to do what I do. So I got out a piece of paper and I started to write. I decided to take what I had learned from my career in financial planning: about assessing where you are versus where you want to be, about setting goals, and about the power of taking the first most natural step. I decided to apply that to this whole idea of a spirit-mind-body connection. And I sat and wrote down "Spirit, Mind, and Body," and where I was and where I wanted to be in each area. That was the first most natural step.

	Where You Are	Where You Want To Be	First Step
Spirit	Crushed	On Top of the World	Talk to Peter
Mind	Fearful/Anxious	Strong and in Control	Get Professional Help
Body	Weak	Strong/Cancer Free	Take the Dog for More Walks

My journey began that day. I knew I was going to need to get comfortable with being uncomfortable. I was going to need to get good at starting over. I wrote down my plan. I began to take the first steps. If something worked, I did more of it. If it didn't, I found something else.

And I went from the couch—wearing a diaper, holding the puppy in the dark, watching old World War II movies that I'd watched with my dad growing up, waiting for the next six hours to go by so I could take another Percocet to kill the pain—to heli-skiing in British Columbia, back on top of the world again. And guess what? It started with taking the dog for a walk. That was the real journey: taking the first step to get up again. If you break things down into manageable pieces, take the first step, and don't quit, you can do anything. But it didn't happen overnight. It would take three long years. The hard work was about to start and I was going to need some help.

Notes of Reflection:

Chapter 6

It's Okay to Ask for Directions

Yes, it is okay to ask for directions. It is okay to get help. Too many of us won't allow ourselves to ask for help. It makes us feel vulnerable, needing help. And we hate feeling vulnerable, because that makes us feel shame. Shame leads to so many bad things: violence, addiction, depression. We need to allow ourselves to ask for help, and be vulnerable, without shame—especially men. Men are not even allowed to ask for driving directions when we are lost. How can we rely on others and get help when we need it? We've got to be able to admit that when something is difficult, it's okay to get help. In fact, not only is it okay to ask for help, it's actually the courageous thing to do—the smart thing to do. So what's wrong with being smart and courageous? My pride had already been torn down. What was there to lose?

When we're sick, we go to the doctor. When our car doesn't work, we go to a mechanic. We have a technology guy at work. We pay for a lawn guy and a plumber. We get all sorts of help from all kinds of people, but needing a shrink? I knew I needed help, so I finally made the call.

Getting Good at Starting Over

Sitting in my office after making my first plan to get up again, I knew what I needed to do. For about three months I had a phone number sitting on my desk for a therapist that a dear friend of mine had given me, and clearly the first thing I needed to do was get out of crisis. I was living every day in fear and crushed by anxiety. The first most obvious step for me was to go to therapy. This was something I'd never done. But I'd been putting it off for too long. I picked up the phone and finally made the call.

Cognitive Therapy

Sitting down with the therapist that first day had me on the edge of my seat and ready to walk out. I had told myself that if the first thing he talks about is medication, "I'm out." I had taken some time to decide what I wanted to get out of going to see him. That's something else I've learned from being an advisor. People come to me and say they need my help and I always ask, "Okay. So what do you need my help with? What do you want to get out of this?"

I decided that I didn't want to spend time talking about my past and my childhood. It wasn't always easy but I was long over it. I just wanted to get out of anxiety and learn some life skills to help me better deal with stress. If I only knew! After several months of crying about the past, we were ready to make some real progress.

I'm not sure if there was ever an official diagnosis, but we believed I was dealing with PTSD. I never talk about that much. (That is something that war veteran's deal with, and to compare what I'd been through to them? I can't do it.) It was hard. It was painful. It was difficult to see any progress. Little by little I learned all the mistakes I was making in my thinking, why that was effecting my emotions, and how it affected my behavior. Little by little I started to gain back some control. Little by little I started to understand myself better and started to avoid those mistakes. Little by little the dark cloud broke

52

apart, and my light started to shine again. Eighteen months later I told the doctor it was time. I'd done what I wanted to do. The anxiety was gone. I had some better skills. It was time to fly on my own.

The journey had begun. During that time and over the next several years, I would continue to try and find things and people that could help me. In many ways it was like continually starting over. Starting something new is never easy. It means giving up control: allowing for changes and learning to let those changes happen. It takes time and patience. Results are not seen every day, every session, or every meeting. We don't see results every bike ride we take right? If there is one thing I've learned from being a financial advisor for eighteen years is that it takes patience and persistence to follow any long term plan. You also have to be able to continually reassess. *Now* where am I compared to where I want to be? *Now* what's the next step? If I was going to get back to the top, I would have to get good at starting over. Here is some of what I tried.

Nutritionist

This was simple and easy. The big thing I got out of this was a plan to eat more of the things that were good for me that I actually liked. It wasn't about adding in a bunch of stuff I did not like to eat; it was about eating more of what I loved that happened to be good for me, too. Brilliant!

Chiropractor

This was a huge step for me. I felt instant results. I felt more energy and had improved overall health. Having energy flow through my spine to where it was meant to be really allowed for me to release years and years of stress and start to feel good again. It was also the first time I had ever gone to a doctor's office, waited to be seen, and walked out feeling better! I actually felt like I was spoiling myself.

Meditation

I'd been using visualization for years. Meditation seemed like the next step. This takes years to master. The best way I heard it explained about learning how to meditate is to just sit down, open your eyes, and watch the show. Don't try to constantly control your mind; just let it be.

Self-help Books

There is so much simple wisdom in the world that we can tap into. Everything we need to know is out there already, including everything in this book; we just have to learn to use it in our own lives. Look for the simple wisdom. You'll know it's true when you find it.

Meeting with a Spiritual Advisor

Knowing that I was also on a faith journey I started to meet on a regular basis with one of my oldest, closest friends who was a priest. Matters of faith can be challenging, and having someone to talk it through with and get advice from was invaluable.

"If comfort is your goal, growth is not in your future."
-Bill Williams

I did all that and more. I bought a road bike and started to ride. I went to a personal trainer and started to get in shape again. I even went to a healer who claimed I was an old soul with amazing powers of transformation. Over and over I'd try new things and came to realize that not only was I getting good at starting over, I was getting comfortable with being uncomfortable.

If your comfort is your goal then growth is not in your future. I learned that quote from a great leader I have the privilege to know in my career in financial services, and I know it to be true. Over and over the things that made me most uncomfortable provided the best opportunity for me to grow. We simply don't grow when we're not challenged. It's when we take a chance and get uncomfortable that we can really learn about ourselves and others. We make mistakes and we learn lessons, and when we can overcome those challenges we grow.

One of the most uncomfortable challenges for me was overcoming sexual dysfunction. I knew going into the surgery for prostate cancer that I would likely suffer sexual dysfunction for up to eighteen months. At eighteen months, the healing is complete and you get a clear picture of the full extent of the issue: will it be permanent or not? As the months went by and the clock was counting down, I was still not functioning well and the pressure started to build. I was trying different medications and combinations. I was trying to eat certain foods to help it along naturally. There were side effects from the medication and frustration from failing time and again. Was I ever going to be healthy and was I ever going to be able to satisfy my wife again?

It may sound sophomoric or immature to some to be so worried about sex, but the truth is, men need to have a healthy sex life to feel strong and confident, and I was willing to try whatever it took. Eventually, having exhausted most of the normal treatments, it was down to two. We could try a powerful form of medication that is injected directly into the penis, or I could have more surgery and have an implant. There was no way I was opting for an implant, so we decided to try the shots. I would need to have the doctor show me how to inject myself and it would take a couple of attempts to adjust to the proper dose. Now here's the thing: I've always been a fainter. When I initially got sick and had my first rectal exam, I fainted. When my beautiful wife Lisa had a miscarriage, I fainted. I'll never forget being in the hospital for the birth of my daughter Sydney, and looking down at my wife's chart and seeing "Caution! Husband is a fainter!" I almost missed the birth because they sent me to get a soda before Lisa started pushing, and I got lost getting back to the room. Yes, this was going to be uncomfortable, but what did I have to lose?

I went in a little nervous and a little excited to potentially have found a fix. Unfortunately, just after the shot, I didn't feel right and it wasn't just that I felt faint and was sweating. My breathing was off and my heartbeat did not feel right. The next thing I knew they were calling 911 so I could go to the hospital, which was just across the street. The police showed up, asking, "What happened? Are you serious?" So I told them I had a shot. "Where?" Ugh. In my penis. "Why?" Sexual dysfunction. Then the ambulance showed up with more, "What Happened?" They took me to the hospital. Then the nurse asked, "What happened?" I had a shot. The PA asked, "Where?" In my penis. The doctor wanted to know, "Why?" Sexual dysfunction. Over and over, all day long, the same questions and the same answers, and I sunk lower and lower, and have never been so embarrassed in my life. I drove home dejected. I'm not having surgery again so this is it. I'm done. I can't fight this anymore, and worry. I'm just going to have to let it go.

And then several weeks later, after really just letting it go and simply accepting what will be, well what do you know? It worked. Sometimes we have to fight and strive, and sometimes when we just have to know when to let it be and stop fighting ourselves, and get out of our own way so we can heal. After we get uncomfortable is when we're given opportunities to grow.

There Really *is* a Strong Spirit-Mind-Body Connection

Little by little, the pieces were starting to fall into place. I had gone to therapy and gotten out of crises. My mind was clear. My body was healing and my sexual function was back. I came to realize that what was once an idea, and what I had questioned to even be true, was starting to prove true in my mind. There is no doubt any more. There *really is* a deep connection between spirit, mind, and body. When one is attacked all three will suffer together, and in order to build up one, we have to build up all three.

Notes of Reflection:

Chapter 7

Find Out What Makes
You Come Alive

I was out of crises and that was great. I had survived, but I didn't just want to survive anymore, I wanted to *thrive*! In fact, I wanted to fly, so Scott and I made it a goal to go heli-skiing when I was officially cancer free. It was still a few years away, but the goal had been set. Often, I found myself thinking about this whole idea that I wanted to thrive again. I was feeling much better, but there was still something missing. One day, I went to church to hear a lifelong friend who was a priest celebrate Mass. During his homily, he read an old quote from Howard Thurman, "Do not ask yourself what the world needs. Ask yourself what makes you come alive, and then go do that. Because what the world needs is people who have come alive."As I sat in the back of church, the simple wisdom in the quote spoke to me and I believed it to be true, and realized that this is what I'd been missing. I needed to really *feel* alive again. I needed to go and find out what makes me come alive.

I'd been thinking about hiring a life coach for some time. Conveniently, one of my clients was also a coach. That would make it uncomfortable for sure. She paid *me* for advice. I would now pay *her* for advice. If she was really going to coach me, I would have to share things that could change how she feels about me and that could affect our relationship. Yes, this was going to be an uncomfortable step. Perfect. It must be the right one! So I hired her and wrote down what I wanted to get out of our time together; my goal was to find out what makes me come alive so I could thrive again.

> *Tip:* People today often remark about how lucky I am to know what my passion is, what my "thing" is (I have several, actually: fishing, skiing, soccer, and a few others). They tell me they wish they could find theirs. I always tell them to think back to when they were kids; what did you love to do most as a kid? Start there. I always loved to fish and ski and play soccer. I did not have to find my passion, I just had to keep it. If you're not a physical person—if it's not a sport or an activity for you—then I would bet your thing is emotional, and most likely revolves around doing things to make others happy, so look there.

The Legacy I was Given

One of the first things we looked at during our coaching sessions was *why* I do the things I do, and how those things aligned with my core values. By that time, I knew how precious our time here was, and I no longer wanted to do anything I didn't *really* want to do! So we completed a core values exercise. In this type of assignment, you begin with a list of core values and you keep removing values until you are left with five *core* values. These are the values we believe to be most important in our lives. Once I got to the point of my five core values, my coach had me boil them down to just two. My core values were *family* and *connection*. These are the things that drive me the most, and conversely, these are the things that when negatively impacted, would bother me the most. This simple wisdom felt so true to me. I'd like to share an exercise with you now (on the following page) to help you find *your* core values.

YOUR IDEAL VALUES WORKSHEET

Instructions:

1. Take a look at the boxes below and cross off the values that you know for certain are not your top values.

2. Take another swipe at the words that are left; continue to cross off the values that would not land at the top of your priority list.

3. With each pass it gets harder to narrow it down, but keep crossing off values until you have your top five.

Service	Friendship	Order	Spirituality	Flexibility	Competence
Play	Stability	Family	Loyalty	Freedom	Integrity
Safety	Status	Meaningful Work	Competition	Community	Leadership
Adventure	Challenges	Change	Worth	Wealth	Recognition
Creativity	Ethics	Education	Relationships	Health	Excellence
Security	Pleasure	Honesty	Privacy	Philanthropy	Religion
Fairness	Environmental Health	Fame	Helping Others	Money	Power
Cooperation	Independence	Diversity	Excitement	Connection	Happiness

Armed with this knowledge, my coach and I started to dig into the different aspects of my life and asked, "*Why?*" *Why* am I a financial Advisor? *Why* do I keep showing back up to this business that for me has not been easy, with my timing always being off? *Why* do I coach (I'm really into coaching soccer)? What's my "*Why*" for being a good father and husband? *Why* do I keep showing up?

On my journey, it had taken tremendous strength and courage to get through each day. I often looked back to gain strength from the legacy I was given. You see, my grandmother got polio when she was five. Her Aunt Flocie—one of my favorite people ever—had pulled her around in a little red wagon when she could not get around on her own. My grandmother went on to beat polio and finish her education. She raised a family and cared for a granddaughter who was born with Down Syndrome, refusing to let her be put into an institution. They told her mother the child would not live two years, but thanks to my grandmother, she lived to be fifty. When my grandmother was in her fifties, her husband died of cancer and she became an executive at Bell Atlantic. This was during the sixties and seventies, when women just didn't do that. And she had financial independence until the day she died, by saving money every time she got paid. My grandmother was strong and determined.

Then there's my Aunt Carol. Her beloved husband Tom died of ALS, leaving behind four children between the ages of four and fourteen. Tom was a truck driver who didn't have great benefits and who had no life insurance, yet I watched my aunt Carol raise my four cousins on love and Social Security checks. And still, she was the most generous person in my life. I learned from her what it meant to be truly generous of heart.

Then there's my dad, who was raised by a single mother on some very mean streets in upper Manhattan. He never knew his own father. He looked out for his little sister and took care of himself. After high school, he enlisted in the U.S. Army. He had nothing but the shirt on his back and a few bucks in his pocket when he got out. Fortunately, he had met my mom, and with the love of my mother, grandmother, and Aunt Carol, he showed up to work every day as a salesman and earned enough to buy his own home and send his two sons to college. On top of that, he found time to be the original Coach Fred—coaching all of our baseball teams. One day soon, when he feels he's ready (he's in his mid-seventies), he may just retire.

So why am I a financial advisor and coach? It's because it matters.

When you need courage and strength, look to the past and the legacy you were given. We're Americans; we all come from a long line of determined, strong people. Tap into that strength and remember, we all have it in us to get up again.

The worksheets on the following pages will help you to better understand who you are, what you do, and why you do it.

YOUR "I AM" WORKSHEET

Instructions:

1. Circle all that apply to you to help define your professional and personal life.

Employee	Coach	Friend	Student	Aunt/Uncle
Manager	Volunteer	Sibling	Artist	Pet Owner
Entrepreneur	Christian	Instructor	Skier	Cyclist
Leader	Spouse	Runner	Golfer	Swimmer
Boss	Child	Teammate	Sports Fan	Wine Enthusiast
Parent	Grandchild	Owner	Musician	Writer
Presenter	Fitness Enthusiast	Yogi	Religious Leader	Foodie

2. Add your own: list other words that describe who you are that are not listed above.

1.	
2.	
3.	
4.	
5.	

YOUR WHY YOU DO WHAT YOU DO WORKSHEET

Instructions:

1. Review your "I AM" worksheet.

2. Pick three to five labels (or more) that describe you.

3. Add a "Because Statement" to each label to help define why you do what you do.

Example:

I am an advisor *because* I watched my aunt struggle to raise my cousins after my uncle's untimely death.

I am	an advisor	because	I watched my aunt struggle to raise my cousins after my uncle's untimely death.
I am		because	
I am		because	
I am		because	
I am		because	

Living Your Legacy

Once we understood my why, we started to talk more about what I was going to do with it all, and one day my coach asked me a very powerful question: "Are you living your intended legacy today, and if not, what are you waiting for?" There was that question again: "What are you waiting for?" As we dug into it a little deeper, the simple wisdom of this question rang true to me. I had learned as a financial advisor that you don't leave a financial legacy if you don't make certain choices about your finances. Financial legacies don't happen on their own. I also believed from coaching kids that there is no "non-impact." In other words, you have an impact on every kid you coach. The question is, will it be a good impact or a bad one (because you're having an impact either way)? Shouldn't it be a positive one?

I had once worried that my legacy was going to be that I was the financial advisor who died too soon, without enough life insurance for his kids. I was now realizing that I *was* leaving a legacy, but maybe not the one I intended to leave. What kind of impact was I going to have? What was my legacy going to be? I began to seriously consider my legacy and what it could be. I thought, "Maybe I can help carry some of the burden for others."

I had never before really looked ahead. I was always trying to deal with and heal from the past. I was always just trying to make it through each day.

It was hard for me to look ahead, so my coach and I had a session where we did what she called a "Future Self Meditation." I was guided by her to the "future," where I walked up to a house I had never seen before, and knocked on the door. It was answered by me, twenty years into the future. We shook hands, and as soon as I saw myself, I started to cry.

I was happy, healthy, successful and *alive*! I had been afraid to look too far into the future because deep down, I was still afraid I would not *have* a future. But to see that it was even a possibility for me to be truly happy and healthy sometime in the future, and that I got to decide what that future would look like, was absolutely amazing. I will never forget that day when I got a glimpse of what it could be like, knowing in my heart that I could make that happen for us all. It was very emotional for me.

Then I was guided to have a conversation where my future self would tell me the most important thing I needed to know to get from where I was, to where I was going to be. My future self told me, "Just keep doing what you're doing. Don't worry so much, and enjoy it."

Wow, there it was. I just needed to keep doing what I was doing and I just needed to enjoy myself. I *was* leaving a legacy, and it was the one *I* chose. I just needed to do what I do and stop worrying about it.

Choosing My Why

What I decided I wanted my legacy to be was that I would have an impact on as many people as I could. There is no greater feeling than having an impact on others. I was reminded of this through my work as an advisor and during the time I spent coaching youth soccer. I came to realize that if you want to get up again after getting knocked down, go out and have an impact on someone else. It's the quickest way up.

Just after the global financial crises, my best friend's parents came in to see me. They were worried about their money and investments. I asked them where they were in relation to where they wanted to be. They felt stuck in New Jersey. Their house was bigger than they needed, and the old gang wasn't around much anymore. Their children and grandchildren lived in Pennsylvania and California. They partly wanted to move, but the real estate market had crashed, and so did the stock market, and they were afraid to touch their retirement money. I told them that I didn't know when the markets would bounce back, but housing was down in California, too. So I asked them, "What if you were able to sell your home here and buy something there that costs less to maintain?" I added, "I know that the stock market is down, but you're sixty-eight and seventy-five. What are you waiting for? This is what you saved for. What if we took a sensible distribution amount and had extra money each month? And if you move to California, you'll be with two out of your three grandchildren, and you never know, maybe your son Jimmy will move out there, too."

They were excited at the idea, put their house on the market, starting taking a monthly income, and then Mr. Hamilton was diagnosed with stage-four colon cancer. He went in for an operation, but the tumor was too big and they could not complete the surgery. They sent him home, wanting to try radiation for six months; maybe it would shrink the tumor enough to try again. It did not look good, but they were tough and undeterred, and kept moving the process forward. For whatever time they had left together, they wanted to be in California with their family.

Mr. Hamilton did his treatments, and after six months, they had a scan to look at the tumor. It was a miracle; they could not even find it! The radiation had worked! They sold their home and found a place in California, moving there with another chance at life! Six months later, their son Jimmy's wife got a job offer a half hour away.

Then, the next thing I knew, I went out there for my annual ski trip. I was at the house—with all of their children and grandchildren, and even the family dog—when Mrs. Hamilton pulled me to the side with a tear in her eye and said, "You know Freddy, none of this would have happened if we had not had that meeting in your office where you asked us, "What are you waiting for?"

Two days later, on the mountain with Scott and Jimmy, I had my first "How lucky are you" moment. I was on the mountain, reflecting on that conversation and thinking, "Man, that felt good. I need more of that." I looked over to see Scott and Jimmy so happy, skiing and riding. Their whole bodies just screamed of *joy*. I looked up at the blue sky and tears started streaming down my face, right past my goggles. I could barely see. I stretched out my arms and gave thanks to God. "How lucky am I to even be here today, God?"

Yes, there is no greater feeling than having an impact on others, and lucky for me, I was a soccer coach. I had been coaching youth soccer for several years, and just when I was beginning my journey after cancer, I was asked by the president of the league to be the coach of the new select travel team for my son's age group. They would be starting the third grade and were seven years old. I thought I was going to be a great coach because I had played soccer and loved it. I could teach them how to dribble and kick and throw the ball. I wanted to be someone's Paul Martin, my soccer coach growing up. I loved playing for him.

We picked the team in the spring. I asked a father I trusted to be my assistant, and we hit the practice field that summer. We had some fun, but we worked hard—on passing and dribbling and playing defense—and that fall we went out on the field and got our butts kicked. Turns out, I wasn't so great. People were upset with me and with our play time, and no one liked to lose.

So I sat with my coach after the season ended, and started my process. Where is the team? Where do I want it to be? What is the first, most natural step? And even more important, *why* am I coaching? Well, I wasn't coaching because we were going to be pro soccer players someday. I was coaching because life was going to kick some of them in the teeth, and I wanted them to have sources of strength to draw from so they could get up when they fell down. So I started to share my story with the parents and players; I shared why I was coaching their sons, and what I wanted them to get out of it. Before long, I was having an impact I never thought imaginable.

There was one boy on the team whose father and stepfather had both left him by the time he was seven and joined the team. He was angry and did not trust adults. Then, one male adult started showing up for him three times a week, just like he said he would. My son Andrew and I sometimes took him for ice cream or a slice of pizza after a game; and we took him fishing. I kept an extra water bottle and sweatshirt in the car for him. I did not do much, really. But by the end of the season his mom looked at me with tears in her eyes because, "He's starting to trust again."

There was another boy on the team who had ADHD, and I got him to do his homework. If he didn't do it, he sat on the bench. I only had to sit him out once. His parents were divorced and his dad was not around enough. Every week I would ask him in front of his mother, "Did you do your Homework?" One day his mom brought me a note from his teacher. He had a great week at school and his teacher wanted to send a note home to his mom, but his mom wanted to show *me* the note. She said it was because, "You're the one that gets him to do his home work. You're the one he listens to."

The next spring, one of the boys was diagnosed with Tourette syndrome, and it was affecting him at school and at home. One night, his mom came to practice and I could tell she was disturbed about something. I asked her what was wrong, and she told me she was distressed because her husband couldn't get away from work to be at practice that night, and her son was upset. I told her not to worry, that it was just one practice, and that she could take him home. But she said, "No Coach Fred, you don't understand. Here at practice he's with you and that's as good as being with us. Right now we are so glad that he is on the team, because his condition doesn't affect him at soccer; at soccer *he comes alive!*"

Wow. What did I do for the boys on the team? I just showed up. I showed up and gave them my all. No, I was not a great coach, but I was a grateful one: grateful that with all the heavy things in my life, at night I could just go down to the field and play a game I loved with fourteen sons. I did not have to worry about the stock market or test results. At the field, I could just worry about Tommy tying his shoes. I loved those boys and they knew it. And guess what started to happen? Yeah, that's right, we started to win! Not every game, but we did start to win.

In the league in which we played, if you won enough games in a season, the next season you could move up flights and play better teams. How cool is it that the boys I coached bought into that goal? We were going to win enough games so we could move up and lose again! It wasn't about coming in first; it was about moving up so we would get uncomfortable again, so we could get better. And it did not happen overnight.

Three seasons later, there we were, playing our last game. If we won, we'd move up, and if we didn't win, we wouldn't. It was tied at half time. I told the boys that if they would just do what they do best, we would win. With five minutes left in the game, one of the twins I coached, Tomer, scored a hustle goal, then Andrew and the boys made play, after play, after play, and we *won!* I found myself jumping up and down on the field.

The parents said they had never seen me jump so high. My son Andrew came running up and jumped into my arms, screaming, *"We did it Dad, we did it! We're going to the B flight!"*

Yes, we were going to the B flight. It may seem like a small thing, but I had never felt so good about any win I had ever had. To see those boys I loved work so hard for so long, and then accomplish their goal, was amazing. There is no greater feeling than having an impact on others, and when you lead with your heart, beyond the game, you can be trusted. When you're trusted, you can have an impact, and when you have an impact, winning is easy.

Notes of Reflection:

Chapter 8

Not Cursed . . . Carried!

I'd made great progress with my plan in terms of my mind and my body, but in many ways I was avoiding the spiritual issue that had been holding me back. I never lost belief in God and I was grateful to still be alive, yet deep down I wondered if I was being punished for the mistakes I had made, or if I was cursed in some way, fated to suffer through life for being less than worthy of all I'd received. I'd been given so much, being raised by a good family with love and support, and having access to a good education. I'd been given several chances to live when I could have died. I'd been given so much and felt I could not ask God for help. How could I ask for more when I'd been given so much already?

Even the Prophet Elijah Fell Down

During this time I would often go to my friend Peter's church instead of my own. It was a chance to see him and I loved hearing him preach. I would sit in the back and often be brought to tears, not knowing why. Deep inside, I was still carrying a great weight. I had met Peter through CYO youth group when I was thirteen. It was before he became a priest. Even though he was several years older than me, we just hit it off. We stayed in touch through college (for me) and seminary (for him). I sang in the choir at his first Mass. As the years went by, he became more than a friend; he was a spiritual advisor and our priest. He married my wife Lisa and I, christened our daughter Sydney, was my son Andrew's godfather, and officiated the burial of my grandmother. Before each and every one of my surgeries, he came to my home, and I would cry my eyes out as he anointed me with holy oil. I would not go to surgery without it. I may have been scared for my body but after Peter came I was never scared for my soul. In many ways he anointed our lives, so it made sense that I was drawn to hear him speak.

One Sunday, there was a reading from the old testament about the prophet Elijah. The people had started to worship false idols and had been lead astray by false priests. The profit came and confronted them. To prove that God's power was greater than the idol's, which in fact had no power at all, he had them soak the wooden idols so that no flame could set them ablaze. He then called down God's power and the idols burned with such intense power that not even ash remained—there was no trace whatsoever, and the people believed. Then the prophet went into the desert, fell to the ground, and could not get up for forty days.

Yes, even the great prophet fell down. I wasn't Elijah and I wasn't super human; I was just a frail, damaged human being. Why was I so hard on myself for getting knocked down? Why would I believe that God would be mad or *angry* at me for being hurt by what I went through? If the profit could be a part of God's power, then fall down in the desert only to been seen again with Moses and the risen Lord after the resurrection, could I not forgive myself?

I Had to Forgive Myself First

The reading had given me hope but I still had one more hill to climb. I found myself thinking more and more about the reading and my journey, and why it all happened to me. Was there some reason? Was I being punished? I had always had a talent and a stage presence. Did I miss my opportunity? Is there something I was supposed to do with all of this? Is that why?

With these questions and more rattling around in my head, I found myself driving up to see Peter one day at lunch. I usually did it just to check in on him and have a quick chat. This time it was different; I *needed* to talk to him. It was time to get some help. It was a Tuesday. I knew his schedule and that he should be there. I walked in and said hello. The ladies at the parish knew who I was and one said, "No problem Freddy, let me get him," only he wasn't there. For some reason he had just left. They asked if I wanted to leave a message. I declined, saying, "I'll see him soon." Driving back to work I passed my own parish and decided to go see one of the priests I like there. Once again, even though they thought he was there—and he should have been—he apparently had mysteriously just stepped out. Did I want to leave a message? No thanks.

I started to walk to the car and looked over at the church. Without knowing why, I decided to go say a quick prayer of thanks. I walked into the empty church, knelt down to give thanks, and it all just started to pour out of me. All the pain and suffering from all those years, all the doubts and fear and self-loathing. It all came gushing out of me in great sobs. Never as an adult had I cried so hard. I looked up and noticed some lady up front cleaning. I tried to pull it together so she would not see me that way, and then the unexplainable happened—I felt two arms wrap around me; I actually felt them holding me tight, urging me to let it all out. It was as if God had been calling me to him, but I had it cluttered up and thought I was being called to talk to the priests. God had being calling me directly to him so his Holy Spirit could wrap his arms around me and heal my soul. In that moment, I knew I was loved and I wasn't being cursed.

I forgave myself that day. I forgave myself for being damaged. This was a profound moment for me because when I forgave myself for being damaged, suddenly I was able to truly forgive the other people in my life for hurting me—for what are they but human and frail and damaged like me? Armed with the knowledge that we're all dealing with life and doing the best we can, how could anyone really hurt me again? It's okay to get knocked down. It happens because we are human, not because we are less than. It happens to us all. No, getting knocked down does not define us. I'm not different or special. We *all* have it in us to get up again. What we do after we get knocked down is what really matters most. And we never really know what that person who may be acting in a way we don't approve of is really going through, what they've been through, or what they are about to have to endure. I found myself almost unable to judge people so harshly anymore and felt compassion like never before.

I Thought I was Crushed, but Found I was Carried All Along

Little by little I shared small pieces of my story and what I had learned with the people I met at the field or at work. It seemed every time I did, it helped them. Something I would say would click with them in some way or give them hope. I started to glimpse that maybe I could do something really good with *all* of it. One day while driving on the highway, I began to think about the "girls"—Liz and Eurelous—who worked for my doctor. A few months earlier, I told them that if there was ever another young patient like me who got diagnosed with prostate cancer, and who wanted to talk to someone, I'd be willing to talk to them. I was thirty-nine when I was diagnosed and the doctor's youngest patient ever, and there was no one for me to talk to. I hadn't heard from them and wanted to remind them.

Just as I thought that when I got back to work, I'd call them, I looked up and saw I was about to pass the exit for their office, and without even thinking I pulled off and went in. I always get big hugs when I'm there. I had young kids when they saved me and we had a special connection. I told them I was there to remind them that if someone needed to talk I wanted to help. They said, "It's great that you're willing," and I said, "No, I'm not willing, I'm *wanting*, and there is a difference." They looked at me kind of strange. Suddenly and unexpectedly, the doctor walked in. We hugged and he asked why I was there. I told him I wanted to help. He said, "It's great that you're willing," and I said, "No, I'm *wanting*, not willing, and there is a difference." Wow, you're right Fred, of course!

Two hours later the phone rang. It was the doctor. He had a young patient who was diagnosed that day and who wanted to talk to me. So I called him right up. I told him I'd been right where he was and I was still here, and everything was going to be okay. He was amazed that I was willing to meet with him that night after work. I called my wife to let her know I would not be home right away, and I went to meet him at a coffee shop. We sat down and started to talk. We were the same age and had the same exact numbers and type of prostate cancer. For him it was powerful to see someone who had been through what he was about to go through, sitting there, happy and healthy. Another survivor's presence can mean so much when we just *show up*.

For the first time ever I sat and told my whole story, about all the surgeries and how I got knocked down and had gotten back up again. He sat there kind of stunned. "You give me so much hope," he said. "If you can go through all of that and stand here today like this . . . ." We sat for a while and talked

79

about his family and my wife and kids. Suddenly, he sat up in his chair and looked deep into my eyes with his eyes open wide. Then he buried his head in his hands and began to weep. I held his arm. He pulled himself together and said he was sorry. I told him it was okay, that was what I was there for, and he asked if he could tell me a story. I said of course he could. He told me that ten years earlier he lived in Columbia and was engaged to a beautiful girl named Claudia. Before they could get married, she got cancer and was very sick. He stayed with her to the end. They were never able to get married and just before she died, she told him that he should not worry because she was going to go to heaven and she was going to look out for him. He shared with me that when he was looking into my eyes, suddenly he saw *her* looking back at him through my eyes. He said it was like I was an angel that had been sent to him, and without thinking I said, "That's because you're in the palm of God's hands right now and I know it, because that was where I was. He carried me by putting people into my life just when I needed it most, and that is why I'm here tonight." I never thought about what I was saying and I never understood until that moment that it was true. I was never cursed or being punished; I was carried all along.

We parted ways and I drove home in a blur, shaken. I walked into the house and there they were: Lisa, Sydney, and Andrew. I found myself staring at all the little pieces that made up their faces and eyes, and I was stunned at how beautiful and perfect they were, and felt as though I was looking at them through someone else's eyes.

Notes of Reflection:

Chapter 9

The Power of Our Stories

I've always been a story teller. Growing up with an Irish heritage, my Grandmother often said I'd kissed the Blarney Stone. I began to realize that what I had always done naturally—telling a good story—had a real power. Stories are powerful because storytelling is in our DNA. For thousands and thousands of years, we told stories, and our greatest leaders have always been great story tellers. We told stories to communicate new ideas, to inspire change, and to engage with others in order to educate and warn. We told stories to celebrate success and most importantly, to emotionally connect. Listening to stories is also in our DNA, and since it is something we have always done, it allows us to relax. We know we don't need to do anything or make any decisions. We also know we need to pay attention because it might be important. We remember stories long after we remember facts. Stories can stop the left brain from seeking more and more facts and allows the right brain to take the lead. The right brain can allow for gray area. The right brain is where we make decisions to trust and to take action. The right brain is where we emotionally connect. There is a huge power to sharing stories. That power is the power to *connect*.

From the Couch to the Top of the World

The final pieces were all coming into place. I was back! Spirit, mind, and body! I was back, and maybe a little better than before. I had one final follow-up blood test for prostate cancer and if I passed it, I would be able to say I was cancer free. I had stopped worrying about the results each time. There was nothing left to do but get the results and go celebrate. Our plans were set. Scott and I would be going deep into British Columbia to a place called Revelstoke to live our dream of going heli-skiing. Revelstoke is the last great place to ski in North America that had yet to be spoiled by modern over-development, and we could not have been more excited. And we were a little nervous, too. Any time you have to give your whole medical history before making a reservation to do something, you know it is serious. We'd be wearing an avalanche back pack with an airbag and a rescue beacon. We'd be taking helicopter safety and avalanche rescue training before being allowed to go up.

We got there all amped, went through the training, and were picked to be in the first group to go up. As the helicopter warmed up and we were strapped into the craft, reality began to sink in as the blade spun faster and faster. Then we were told we needed to get out; that we weren't going up that day. The avalanche risk was too high.

The next morning we went through it all over again. We were in the helicopter with the blades spinning. The anticipation grew as the blades spun even faster and just when we thought they couldn't spin any quicker, we were up! It climbed so high so fast, with the winds buffeting the chopper. Scott and I looked at each other with wide-opened eyes. The pilot and guide didn't notice at all, and the next thing we knew we were landing right at the top of the mountain, in an old growth forest with massive trees all around. They're gonna land it *here*?

Yes, it landed. We didn't jump out—that's only for the movies. We got out and hunkered down next to the helicopter, and it took off right over our heads. We rushed to get our skis on as we stood waist deep in snow. We each put on an avalanche back pack, securely strapped it, and removed the handle you pull if you're in an avalanche. Then off we went, through the old growth forest without a trail, making one or two turns, ducking under a tree, dropping ten feet to a small cliff . . . it was crazy and it was awesome.

I thought I was an expert skier before that day. When we got up there, though, I realized there was another entire level and we were right in the thick of it. The first day was a blur, starting with the helicopter landing then taking off right over our heads, followed by the small avalanche I was in where I fell head first into a tree well that morning. That's two of the three ways people often die up there. Now, I know what you may be thinking: you almost die twice and you have to go do *that* to celebrate?

We made it through the first day. I think we were a little shell shocked; that was nuts! Then day two came, with sunny skies and better conditions. We were comfortable. That was the day. We made fourteen trips up and down, doubling the number of runs the other groups did. After lunch we went higher than we had been before, way higher. The pilot took it down on the very top of the mountain on a tiny little spot. It didn't even look big enough. We got out and hunkered down. The helicopter took off over our heads. And there it was: the view from the top of the world! "Holy Cow!" "Oh my God!" Now *this* looks like the website!

There I was at the top of the world, captivated by the most beautiful view I had ever seen, and it hit me: "I did it!" "I did it?" YES, I did it! I had gone from the couch—wearing a diaper in the dark, taking Percocet, holding the puppy, just waiting for the next six hours to go by so I could kill the pain—to the top of the world. And I knew I needed to share our story with more people.

Went Looking for Freddy, Found Coach Fred

Yes, *our* story, not mine. I'm not the only one who has been through adversity. Haven't we all? I'm not the only one who went through ten years of turmoil feeling the effect of the global financial crises and 9/11. That impacted all of us. And I'm not the only one saying, "Great, I survived, and now I want to thrive!" Isn't that what the whole country has been saying for years? No, it's not *my* story, it's *our* story, and I knew I needed to share it.

I needed to share that I had gotten knocked down and gotten back up; that I'm not special or different because we all have it in us to get up again; that I had gone searching for Freddy the happy, confident guy I was when this all started, and he was Gone! In his place I found Coach Fred, who is a grateful husband and father, youth athletic coach, financial advisor, and cancer survivor. I realized I wanted to be a voice for adaptive families—families that can continue to move forward regardless of a changing reality, and go from where they are today to where they really want to be.

So I decided to make a video and share my story for the first time with a bigger audience, and I had no idea how sharing my story would change my life forever.

Top of the World to Center Stage

A few weeks after my trip, I sat down with a friend who had been a producer for television, and together we made my first video. In it I shared the basic raw story of what it was like for me, my wife, my children, the kids I coach, and my clients as I learned I had cancer and fought it, and what it's like now that I beat it. Behind it we put music and footage of the helicopter landing at the top of the world and me saying, "Oh my God, oh my God," as I first saw the view. At the end of the video I announce for the very first time, "I'm Coach Fred."

It took us all day to create the video, and then my friend had to put it all together. I went home feeling good. The following day I returned to see the completed video. I was amazed. Driving back to my office that day I was suddenly overcome with emotions—tears streaming down my face. *I had my answer*! Here was the answer to the questions I had been asking over and over again. This is what I was supposed to do with my talent and this is *why*! This is why I had to go through what I went through, so I could now help other people.

The video began to get shared on social media. People loved it and started to react to it. They wanted to know where the book was and where the movie was. They wanted to know, "Are you going to make more videos?" A few days later I met with a leader from the company in which I own a franchise. I shared it with him and he loved it! He wanted to know if he could share it. He saw opportunities I didn't even see, and the next thing I knew I got an email from the president of the largest financial planning firm in the country. It read: "Hi Coach Fred, I'd love to hear your story."

A few days later I was in Manhattan sharing my story, and I got asked to give a speech at a conference for top women financial advisors. So I went down to Maryland and gave a speech to a group of amazing women, and they laughed and cried with me. At the end of my talk they stood up and cheered, and it was awesome!

For one day I was a motivational speaker and it was pretty cool, and for me it was enough. But the executive VP was there and heard me speak. The next day I received an email from him telling me to "Strap in," that my life had changed. He wanted me to be the keynote speaker at their national leadership conference. I did it, and a room full of great leaders laughed and cried and cheered. The next thing I knew I was a national motivational speaker, flying across the country sharing my story with thousands of people. Once again, I was having an impact I never thought imaginable, and it was the most incredible time of my life.

When we take a risk to be vulnerable and share our stories from the heart, it connects us with everything valuable.

Notes of Reflection:

Chapter 10

One Hill at a Time

Yes, suddenly my entire life had changed, and in order to adapt to this changing reality, I was going to need to take everything I'd learned about transformation to a whole new level. I had to make room in my life to be Coach Fred for more people and adjust to a brand new persona I was building; I was going to need to transform my business and coaching, my family life, and all of my routines. Suddenly, I needed a website and logo, business cards, and . . . a book? I was traveling and away from my office. I needed a bigger staff and someone to plan my travel. I needed more help with my soccer team. I couldn't stop coaching or leave my financial planning practice. I wasn't looking to blow up our whole life, just find the time and space to do more so I could have a purpose and be happy. This was going to be a big mountain to climb. I was going to have to change everything, yet change nothing when it came to my commitment to my family and clients and soccer team. I was out telling others to keep showing up for what matters most in their lives. What would I be if I didn't coach anymore, or wasn't an advisor or a present father? I'd be just another motivational speaker and there are thousands of those. Thankfully, my journey and my love for skiing had taught me one very important lesson: each mountain is climbed one hill at a time.

The Day After My Life Changed

The day after I went heli-skiing, my life was changed and I didn't even know it yet. I was given an experience that I would later use as a "guide" for my journey—a guide for transformation.

My buddy and I knew that we needed to go right back to a regular ski resort and ski off the lifts. Life wasn't all heli-skiing and we did not want to spoil our love of just being on a "regular" mountain. We were still all fired up from the two days in the helicopter and were definitely looking for a rush. Lucky for us, at the very top of the mountain after the last lift, you could hike up another 150 yards, get to the back side of the mountain, and drop off into the back bowl. We took off our skis and hiked up. When we got to the very top and were putting our skis back on, a member of the ski patrol came up behind us and very carefully inched up to a small space between a giant rock on one side and a cliff on the other. Then, he disappeared into the unknown. My buddy Scott is the real expert skier so he went first and inched up, disappearing into the unknown. I thought, "Well, I climbed all the way up here and I'm not going to climb down now," so I too dropped off into the unknown.

We ended up on a tiny, three-foot wide ledge. There was a giant snow storm on the back side and it was whiteout conditions. You couldn't see a thing. The back bowl is what's left of an old, blown out volcano. The mountain went straight up above us and straight down beneath us so we had no choice but to keep heading around on the ledge. Eventually, we saw that the ski patrol tracks headed down the mountain so we turned down. But we still couldn't see, so we were forced to make one turn and stop, then make one turn. We were essentially skiing blind, reacting to what our feet were telling us. One turn. Stop. Check for each other. Make one turn. Stop.

Eventually, we got down into the trees where we were able to get some depth perception, and then it was awesome! We made turn after turn, flying through the trees. This was just what we came for, *whew*! The next thing we knew, we were at the bottom of the run. If we wanted the ride to continue, we needed to do the hard work to get all the way to the top again.

This would become a guide for the journey I would go on. First, I made the video and shared it. I had dropped off into the unknown. Next, I was asked to give a speech. I was moving along the ledge not knowing where I was going. Then, I had more speeches and needed a business with a logo and website. I did not really know what I was doing yet and was making one turn by instinct, then stopping, then taking the next step. Then it started getting fun. One opportunity led to the next and the next and the next. Each time I had to climb a new hill and face a new challenge. And it wasn't until I had climbed each hill that I was able to see the next one to climb. You can't see the path to the top when you are standing at the bottom.

If You Look at the Tress You're Gonna Hit the Trees

To both go through adversity and truly transform, you have to focus on the opportunities, not the obstacles. When I went heli-skiing and shared it with the boys I coached, they were like, "Wow coach, that's awesome! But what kind of trail do you ski on?" I told them that we don't ski on a trail, we ski through the trees. "How do you ski through the trees, coach?" Well, you never look at the trees. If you look at the trees you're going to hit them every time, because your body follows your head and your head follows your eyes. Whatever you focus on is what you're going to hit. You have to look at the space between the trees. In that space there will be an opportunity to turn, and that space will lead to the next turn and the next and the next.

And when you're really going good, you're not looking down at the turn you're currently making; you're looking three turns down the hill.

If we focus only on the obstacles in our life, we'll hit them time and time again. We have to focus on the opportunities. That means that when we're dealing with adversity or health issues, we must focus on the thing we can still do, not the things we can't. When I was recovering from surgery and couldn't play sports or go fishing, I started gardening. It gave me something to do and to focus on instead of focusing on all that I couldn't. Before I knew it I had lots of cucumbers, so I learned how to make pickles! One opportunity led to the next.

When you're trying to transform your life, you have to look for the opportunities to get uncomfortable and make change. When you're trying to have an impact on others, you have to look for the opportunities to connect. We have to focus on opportunities, not obstacles.

The other things I told them about heli-skiing was that first, you'd better be good and it takes practice. We have to develop life skills. Second, you need to have the right equipment. For skiing, that's skis and a helmet, but in life that's the right attitude and emotional competence. And the last thing I told them is that you never go alone. Yes, that's right! You never go alone because even when you focus on the opportunities and not the obstacles, sometimes you're going to crash, and you'll need help getting up, so you never go alone. It's the same for life. We can't do it alone.

Transformation (Fred's Mountain Model)

Armed with this knowledge, I began to enhance the Sprit-Mind-Body plan I'd started to create. We need hope in our lives. It allows us to see that the future could be different and better than today. But hope is not enough. We have to plan to be successful and plan for happiness. We need to plan how we're going to have an impact and what our legacy will be. It is not enough to hope to have health, is it? No, we have to plan for all of these successes in our life.

So I started to add pieces to the plan and started to apply the process of assessment to the rest of my life. I looked at my financial planning practice and asked, "Where is it? Where do I want it to be? What's the first step?" I also looked at my soccer team, my speaking business, and my relationships, and found I could break each piece down even further. Website? Logo? Then I added still another question: "What will my impact be?" There is no greater feeling than having an impact on others.

I also found that it was helpful to identify what was going well. What were the things I wanted to keep doing, and do more often? I found that in most areas of my life, there were a lot of good things happening and I wanted to make sure I kept doing them. I also took time to identify what the challenges were. These are the things we want to be aware of but not focus on. These are the obstacles. I found that in order to make room to do more of the things that were working, I needed to remove some habits or routines. Often, these were the obstacles and they just needed to be removed to make more space for the opportunities—for more of the good. I found that by adding into my life more and more of the activities, habits, and routines that were good for me, my team, or my business, eventually they would completely outweigh the negatives or challenges I faced. This was true of meeting with a nutritionist, or therapist, or life coach. This is true when I meet with a new client: we start with making sure we don't change what is working for us.

I began to realize that we all need to begin with *Sprit-Mind-Body* as the foundation for health in our lives. That's the foundation we need in order to survive. But for us to *thrive*, many other pieces must come together. And we are all unique, so for each of us to truly come alive, our individual mountains will look different. When Mother Theresa was in India doing her amazing work, people would come and ask her how they could help in Calcutta and she would tell them to "Find your own Calcutta."

For me it was coaching my children, and fishing and skiing with my loved ones. For me it was financial planning and motivational speaking. We're not all called to write a book; we are called to live a full and meaningful life and help those around us when we can, in the way we can. We are called to show up with *all* of who we are.

Transformation Model

Just as climbing a mountain is completing a series of hills and valleys; transformation is making changes over time; mastering each goal, gaining momentum, overcoming plateaus and handling setbacks.

Reaching each peak builds momentum to get through the next valley. Completing each goal along your journey adds learning and understanding to handle setbacks as you climb toward your next goal. The journey unfolds as you move forward. Once you've climbed the first hill, the next peak reveals itself.

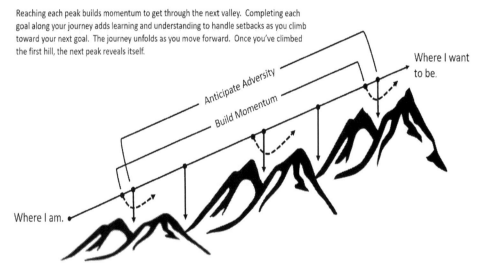

Where I want to be.

Anticipate Adversity

Build Momentum

Where I am.

When we set out on a journey to transform our life or our business or our health, we have to remember that each mountain is climbed one hill at a time as we start the journey to the top. You can't see the whole path to the top. Initially, it will seem difficult as we climb, but once we get up that first hill we will begin to gain some momentum. Then, we can glimpse the next hill or even the next journey.

There will be times when we'll plateau or hit a valley—more adversity and change. Eventually, we will begin to climb the next hill of the next challenge and once again, we'll have to do some hard work and get uncomfortable to move forward. On and on this will be the journey of our lives. There will never be an end—only new beginnings and opportunities to grow, learn, and ultimately transform, so we can live fuller, more meaningful lives.

The worksheet on the following page might help you think about how you could transform some of the areas in your life. Have fun with it. For a printable version of this worksheet that you can use again and again, visit Coach-Fred.com/worksheet.

Transformation Worksheet

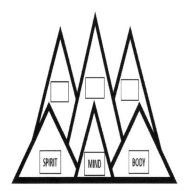

Step 1:
Begin with Spirit, Mind & Body; then consider the additional parts of your life that you want to transform. Label the other peaks in the mountain model above.

Step 2:
Answer the 6 questions for each label
1. Where am I?
2. Where do I want to be?
3. What's my first step?
4. How can I have an impact?
5. What do I want to do more of?
6. What challenges do I want to remove?

▲ SPIRIT
1.	2.	3.
4.	5.	6.

▲ MIND
1.	2.	3.
4.	5.	6.

▲ BODY
1.	2.	3.
4.	5.	6.

▲ _____
1.	2.	3.
4.	5.	6.

▲ _____
1.	2.	3.
4.	5.	6.

▲ _____
1.	2.	3.
4.	5.	6.

Notes of Reflection:

Chapter 11

Survive and Thrive

My journey started when I decided that I did not want to *survive* anymore, I wanted to *thrive*. I thought that it was black and white and very cut and dry; you were either surviving life or you were thriving, but you didn't do both, or so I thought. I guess I had one more lesson to learn.

There's never a good day to get cancer...again!

By the spring of 2014 I had done it. In two amazing years, I had pretty successfully transformed my life so I could keep doing all the things I loved and find the space to add in the thing that made me come alive—being Coach Fred for more people and sharing my stories to help others connect the dots in their lives. I used my process and the "guide for transformation" that I received the day after I went heli-skiing, and I was really on top of my world again. But you see, I had forgotten about the last part of that day on the mountain: that all of a sudden, just when everything was going great and we were flying through the trees, the run ended, and we had to do the hard work to climb up the mountain again. Sitting in the doctor's office, having just posted on social media that I was waiting for the results of my six-year PSA and was about to be six years cancer free, I got the bad news. My PSA was up, and being that I had my prostate removed, I should not have a number at all. "Can't believe I made that post." They would take another sample to make sure the results were accurate. They told me not to worry and to come back in two weeks. I posted that there had been a mistake with the results. My head said don't get ahead of yourself, but my gut told me this was bad.

Back at the doctor's office alone, it was a Tuesday. I had told my wife "I got this, go to work." The results were accurate. The cancer was back. Again? Really? But...I did all the right things! But...I'm Coach Fred, cancer survivor. "So when do we begin the radiation, doc?" I called my wife, my parents, and my best friend Scott, from the parking lot. In a daze, I went back to work. I sat down at my desk and asked myself, "What are you going to do?" I sat there for a while and said to myself, "You're Coach Fred and you're an expert at adversity!" Then I cleared off my desk, got out a piece of paper and a pen, and began to plan.

I Had to Take My Own Advice

Yes, an expert at adversity and I was going to need to take my own advice. So I started to write: *Where am I? Where do I want to be? How am I going to continue to have an impact?* I knew I wouldn't be able to go out on the road and speak when I was home doing treatments every day. *Who am I going to need to share this with?* I thought, not only do they deserve to know, but I'm going to need their support. We can't do it alone.

It's never too early or too late to make a plan. The first time I had cancer I waited two years and until I had collapsed before making a plan. This time I waited two hours, and it took those two hours to admit to myself that, *"This sucks!"* It's okay to take a moment and admit that something is going to be hard— that it will be difficult. If we can't admit it is difficult, how can we truly fight it? How can we get the right help?

The next day, I began to make the calls, to share the news and let people know I had a plan. It was amazing, really. The

102

first time I had cancer I called my parents and my best friend. This time I had so many new people in my life and had to make fifteen to twenty calls. I shared the news with Brian Mora, a great friend I had met on my journey. As I shared and told him I had a plan, he gave me the words I really needed. He said, "You know, Fred, don't take this the wrong way, but if this was anybody else, I'd be devastated. But I've got to tell you, I don't feel bad for you. I feel bad for the cancer because it's about to get its butt kicked!"

Yes, our words are so important, and I decided that in order to continue having an impact on others, I'd make a video each Friday and share how I was using what I learned in the past to battle cancer again. I told the world in the first video that my cancer was back but don't feel bad for me because cancer was going to get its butt kicked. Every day, I would leave work, put on the war paint, commit my spirit, mind, and body to healing, and I would visualize my way through each treatment. I avoided the "emotional hand grenades," those opportunities to get angry and frustrated when tests were delayed or vacation plans and speeches were canceled. On Fridays, I made my videos and continued to have an impact, and I started to realize that it wasn't survive or thrive, it was survive *and* thrive. When it started again, I thought I'd have to survive for a while, doing the hard work, before I could thrive again. But this time, through connection and impact, I found I was thriving while I was surviving treatments.

It's not always one or the other. We can do both. To live a fuller more meaningful life, we have to learn to see the perfection in our imperfect lives, allowing for flaws in ourselves and those around us. We need to embrace all of it, the good times and the bad, and allow connection to be our driving force.

The treatments were finished at the end of July. I took the month of August to rest up and vacation. In September, soccer started and I went back on the road sharing our story. I did not know if the cancer was gone but I was going to live each day to the fullest and have the greatest impact I could. I was running my practice and flying across the country, sharing the story with thousands of people, taking red-eyes home so I could make all the soccer games. And just before Thanksgiving, we got the news: the treatments had worked. We'd done it again!

A Time to Come Home

Yes, we'd done it again. I went through the holidays with tear-filled eyes that year—a constant, "How Lucky am I?" moment. In the end, 2014 had turned out to be a great year, and as 2015 came around I found myself exhausted. I sort of ran myself into the ground. I was grateful, but I had no energy. So I got out a pen. *"Where am I? Where do I want to be?"*

Home! I want to be *home*. I had been telling other people to "Show up with all of who you are for what matters most in your life," and it was time for me to once again take my own advice. What matters most to me is all the people in my life, and the reason I say it's *our* story not *my* story is because I'm not the only one that has faced adversity and had trauma in life. I'm not the only one who went through turmoil and said I wanted more. Haven't we all? And I'm not the only one who got knocked down and got up again. No. And we all have it in us to get up again. But more than anything, I say it's *our* story because I could not have done it without all the amazing people in my life.

It was our family and friends and neighbors who kept the phone always ringing and the mailbox always full. They watched and fed our children and shoveled our snow. It was the doctors and nurses and assistants who caught my cancer early and saved my life. They held me with kid gloves the entire time, because I'm a horrible patient and don't forget, a fainter! It was the other advisors I shared office space with. When my intestines had ruptured and I was struggling to pay the bills, they paid my rent for two months to keep me in business. It was my best friend, Scott, who on the day I got cancer, went home and cried with his wife Jenn and then got on the phone and doubled his cell phone minutes because, "Freddy is going to need to talk." It was my dear friend, Father Peter, who anointed me before every surgery. Because of him, I may have been afraid for my body but never fearful of my soul. It was the kids I coached, their parents, and my clients for letting me in. It was the grandfather of one of my boys that crawled over 1000 feet of stone, praying for me, and sent home a sacred medal with a note "For Coach." It was my Aunt Carol who loved me unconditionally and taught me to be generous of heart. It was my grandmother who set the tone for life, that you work hard and play hard and give back to others when you can. It was my father, who changed the whole future of our family's lives. It was my mother, who told me over and over again, "You can do anything if you don't ever quit." It was my children, Sydney and Andrew, who bring purpose and meaning to my life, and it was my beautiful wife Lisa, who stood with me in church, having no idea what she was about to get into, and vowed to be with me in good times and in bad times, for rich or for poor, in sickness and in health, and then she showed up every day and did just that.

The story is the story of all the people in my life. They did so many little things they will never remember, and that I will never forget. There is no gift of ourselves that we can give that is too small. It was time for me to be home so I could rest and be fully healthy again so I could show up with all of who I am for what matters most in my life.

I'm Coach Fred, and I want you to keep showing up with all of who you are, to what matters most in your life. Remember, you don't have to be more. You are enough as you are. Find out what makes you come alive. Share your passions, connect and have an impact, and you'll go from where you are today to where you really want to be.

Notes of Reflection:

Chapter 12

Show Up With All
of Who You Are

So I went back at it. I was running my financial planning practice, coaching my team, loving my time with my wife and kids, fishing and skiing, and loving my life. It was the summer of 2016 and one day I got a call from someone who had seen me speak several years before. He wanted to tell me a story. He was home one night with his wife, and they were upset. Something was wrong with their daughter who was away at school. They knew something just wasn't right with her. She wasn't herself with them and her communication was way off. They feared the worst but had no idea what to do. They had been agonizing for weeks but that night he looked at his wife and asked if he had ever told her about Coach Fred. He told his wife that Coach Fred would say, "If you don't know what to do and don't know what to say, just show up." So he left home and drove three hours across the state on a Monday night. He went to his daughter's dorm and her roommate told him where she was. He found his daughter and said, "I don't know what to do and I don't know what to say, but I love you so I showed up." She fell into his arms sobbing that she was in real trouble and needed his help; she was becoming addicted to meth. They took her home just in time. She went to therapy and got her life back together. Then she went back to school and graduated. During the call he told me they were just about to celebrate some more! She was getting married. Her future was bright. He wanted to thank me and let me know how my message had impacted his family in this amazing way. He said, "You've got to keep doing what you're doing, Fred. It matters."

This wasn't the only story. I was hearing them time and time again. My message had an impact—sometimes years later—and these were just the ones I knew about. How many more stories were out there that I would never know about? I really love the idea of the unknown. I knew what I needed to do. It was time to write a book and share the simple things I'd learned. So here it is.

By learning to tap into the simple wisdom that's all around us, we can create a fuller and more meaningful life. The biggest thing I've learned is that it's not only important to show up in life but to also show up with all of who you are. It's not only important to show up for the people who matter most in your life, but to also create meaningful connections. Here's how you do that:

Tips to Not Only Survive, but to *Thrive*

1. ***Remember that where you are today is not where you'll always be.***

   If life is going great we need to celebrate every single minute of it! YES! Take time to celebrate the great events in our life, but also remember to cherish and celebrate the little things, too. They fly by way too fast. Don't blink. And remember that every day is a gift and tomorrow your whole world could come crashing down. So today, if you're not where you want to be, or if life has knocked you down, have *hope*, because where you are today is *not* where you'll always be. You get to decide where you go from here, and believe me, if you create deep and meaningful connections in your life, your future may be unimaginably great for you.

2. *Attitude is everything and the only thing!*

When real adversity hits and you can't control anything around you, remember that you do get to control the most important thing: your own attitude. How great is that? So are we going to choose to be a victim, or are we going to choose to be a warrior? You've got to choose to fight for yourself and keep moving forward. The words we choose to use not only towards others but also towards ourselves truly sets the tone of our attitude. Choose your words wisely!

3. *There is a deep Spirit-Mind-Body connection.*

At the core, we are connected. If our body is under attack with a sickness or stress and it lasts long enough, our mind and spirit will be attacked as well. As we build up or fall down, all three move together, so we have to focus on all three. Hope is not enough; we need to plan. Build a Spirit-Mind-Body plan.

4. *Transformation requires a willingness to get uncomfortable*

We don't like change. It makes us uncomfortable, and yet to truly transform we need to make small changes over and over again. We've got to get comfortable being uncomfortable if we want to grow. A dear friend and mentor of mine puts it this way, "If comfort is your goal then growth is not in your future." Taking a risk is nothing more than reaching for an opportunity. What are you waiting for?

5. *Focus on the opportunities, not the obstacles.*

Our body follows our head, and our head follows our eyes. We go where we focus our sight. In order to go from where we are to where we really want to be, we have to focus on the opportunities and take them. One opportunity will lead to the next, which will lead to the next, and so on. If we focus on the obstacles in our lives, one will lead to the next, and we'll hit them again and again. The most important opportunity we can focus on is creating meaningful connections with the people in our lives.

6. *It's okay to ask for help.*

We simply can't do it alone. I would have never gotten through everything I went through without all the other people in my life. Too often, we fear being vulnerable and asking for help. We feel shame and somehow feel "less than" when we need others, as though we need to say "We're fine, everything is okay." But how can we truly fight something if we can't even admit how hard it is, and get help? We can have a great attitude, we can be strong, and we can ask for help. For the *men* reading this, it's okay to ask for directions; you don't always have to know where you're going and how to get there.

7. *How we go into adversity is how we come out.*

If we go into adversity angry and bitter, we will stay angry and bitter. It's like a tight spiral of emotions feeding on itself. If we go into adversity with some patience, and accepting of what we can't control, we will emotionally move away from the trauma and heal faster than we would if we're angry.

8. *Sharing our passions brings us right into the moment.*

Simple wisdom tells us to live in the moment. It sounds so easy, but it isn't. It takes time and it takes practice. What I've found for me is that sharing our passions—the things we love to do most—with others, is the key. When I'm fishing with my son, or skiing with my daughter on the mountain, or cooking a family meal with my hands, it takes me right into the moment. I don't have to think about it or try at all; it just falls into place and I'm right there, fully in the moment. Life's little doubts and fears and stresses will creep back in, but the more we share our passion, the more often we're taken right into the moment. Soon, it starts to become a habit and starts to happen more and more often, and the next thing you know you're going from moment to moment to moment, and the cycle begins again. Share what you love to do most with the people you love most and you will live more in the moment.

113

9. *Understand and articulate your WHY.*

People say it's who you know. I think it's who knows *you*. The people who really know you and know *why* you do what you do are the people who will really help you. People who know your *why* will advocate for you and get on board. People who understand *why* you lead, will follow. Before we can share our *why* and articulate it, we have to understand it. Start by asking yourself, *Why?* for everything you do. *Why do I do what I do? Does this align with my core values?* In this way, we learn to show up with all of who we are with all of our imperfection. When we show up and are vulnerable with others, we give them the permission and inspiration to be vulnerable too.

10. **Lead with your heart.**

I didn't coach soccer because the kids I coached were going to play professional soccer some day; I coached soccer because I knew life was going to kick some of them in the teeth some day, and I wanted them to have the strength to get up again. So I started to coach them beyond the game of soccer: for the bigger game, the game of life. The next thing I knew I was being trusted, which allowed me to have an impact. Once I was able to have an impact on their lives, we started to win. When you lead with your heart—beyond the game—you can be trusted. When you're trusted, you can have an impact on the people you lead. When you have an impact, you'll get hard work, dedication, and loyalty, and when you get that, winning will be easy!

114

11. Choose the legacy you leave by the way you live today.

As a financial advisor, I have many conversations with people about their legacy. I remind them of something I learned from a coach I had, which is that you don't get to leave a legacy without first living it. It's the decisions we make today and the manner in which we live our lives that ultimately decides the legacy we leave, whether that be a financial legacy or our life's legacy. You don't get to leave a legacy without first living it. What is your intended legacy, and are you living it today?

12. Connection is the driving force in our lives.

Connection allowed me to survive, and connection with others allowed me to thrive. When I was knocked down again and again, it was the people in my life who showed up for me over and over again—in big and small ways—that drove me forward. They did things for me they will never even remember, but that I will never forget. There is no gift we can give of ourselves to others that is too small. When we are connected and having an impact, we can do more than survive; we can survive and *thrive* at the same time.

13. Find out what makes you come alive.

There is an old quote by Howard Thurman that has had a bigger impact on me than possibly any other learning on my journey:

"Don't ask yourself what the world needs. Ask yourself what makes you come alive and then go do that. Because what the world needs is people who have come alive."

Happiness is underrated. We all deserve to feel *alive*.

14. Keep showing up with all of who you are.

If you don't know what to say and you don't know what to do for someone in your life, just show up! Often, the most important thing we have to offer someone is our presence. When we show up, we have an opportunity to have an impact that we never even imagined. There is no gift too small that we can offer someone else, and no matter what happens in our lives, we have the opportunity to not just show up, but to show up with all of who we are. If we just keep showing up every single day with all of who we are, then our futures will be unimaginable.

Notes of Reflection:

117

Epilogue

The Bigger Big Picture

As time has passed, I've had more and more people in my life, and in the lives of the people around me, who lost their battle and don't get to have a happy ending. Too many don't get to be a "Cancer Survivor." They suffer and then they die. Their struggle and their pain takes a toll on their closest family and friends and their loss leaves a hole in our hearts that can't be filled. Too often, there are unresolved issues and regret. Yet the sun comes up each day and we're called to get up, move forward, and continue to live.

What I've learned is that we don't get to choose the hour or the manner of our death; we only get to choose how we face it. We don't get to choose when or how our loved ones die. Again, we only get to choose how we face it. As it is in life, in death we get to choose how we show up.

After we lost yet another family member, my daughter asked me how I've learned to deal with it. I told her that first off, I have my faith which is a message of hope, and second, I view it as a choice. We can have many people we love in our life and that will bring tremendous joy, and at times, tremendous pain.

The alternative is a life without many people in it. We won't have much pain, but how much joy? No, I choose to take the pain as a price for tremendous joy. I believe we all deserve a life of joy. We all deserve to really live and I think we only get to do that when we have real connection.

People talk about the need to "Live like you're dying" and I agree. Life is fragile. We are all going to die.

We should not wait to live the life we want—to live life to the fullest. It's why I wrote this book. And it does make for a great country song, no? So YES, live like you're dying. But ask yourself this: what would our relationships and life be like if we all loved like *they're* dying? What if we loved the people in our life like we knew they were dying and showed up for them every day while they're living, in the same way we do when they're dying? For sure we'd have less regrets. We'd have fewer families broken up, less grudges being held, and way fewer relationships to fix before it's too late. Would you forgive more freely if they were dying tomorrow? Would you love more fully? Would you make more time to just be able to spend a little bit more of it with them? Would you listen to them more? Would you make sure to be in the moment and really be connected? Would you go out of your way to help them? Would you just show up even if you don't know what to say or do or what they need? If we love like they're dying, we'll also be more likely to be at peace when they're gone, having more memories to treasure and honor, and the sure knowledge that we loved them to the fullest when we were here together. And when in the end it is their time to go, do we make it about them or about us? Do we make it about how their sickness or dying hurts us, or do we show up for them and only them knowing we'll have time to heal later?

And how do we show up for those who are left here to grieve? Do we show up at all? Often we show up in force when someone first dies or gets sick but as the weeks go on, it seems we go back to our lives too quickly. Maybe we just don't show up anymore because we don't know what to say or what to do, so it sort of lets us off the hook.

In order to keep showing up for someone else, you have to just show up *once* for God's sake. Could you take in a garbage can or shovel the snow? Could you drop off a pizza or cut some flowers and bring them over? Could you drop a card in the mail? We don't have to know what to do or what to say. When we show up with an open heart the impact we can have or the little thing we can do will present itself—it will unfold—and it just may be the little act of kindness they really needed. You never really know the impact you can have until you just show up and see. And then all you need to do is show up again and again and then it will become more than a habit: it will become a lifestyle, where all you do is show up with all of who you are.

COACH FRED

To book Coach Fred for speaking or to contact him, please use the email address below:

Fred@coach-fred.com

About Fred Schuldt

Looking back, Fred Schuldt was already considered by some to be an inspirational leader and gifted storyteller, traits that came in handy during his seemingly normal life of trials and triumphs as a loving family man, successful executive, and admired coach. But it took the impending loss of that life to truly forge these talents—giving them purpose while giving their bearer perspective.

Like many others, Fred was forced to face cancer and its life-threatening complications, and like some others (though never enough), he survived. His decade-long story of survival recounts not only the debilitating blows of the disease and Fred's four major surgeries, but also the depression of one so sick while so young, and that young man's struggle with other life challenges against the backdrop of terminal illness. Fred's experiences during his ascension from rock-bottom toward the peak of personal achievement embody the literal meaning of "life lessons."

Now with cancer in his rear-view mirror—having been beaten down with sickness and built back up with spirit—

Fred channels his social and motivational skill set toward inspiring others. His mission is to arm those around him with the personal skills and inner strength to face adversity before it strikes, to recognize what really matters, and realize life's attainable dreams. Fred wants to share in the silver lining that his wake-up call with cancer provided, because it shouldn't take the risk of losing one's life to truly begin living that life to the fullest.

Keep Showing Up!

Splendor Publishing's life-changing books are written by skilled and passionate leaders, entrepreneurs, and experts with a mission to make a positive impact in the lives of others.

Splendor books inspire and encourage personal, professional, and spiritual growth. For information about our book titles, authors, or publishing process, or for wholesale ordering for conferences, seminars, events, or training, visit SplendorPublishing.com.

Made in the USA
Middletown, DE
08 February 2019